J.C. LEVINSON - GUERILLA MARKETING

PAGE 19

"WHISPERING LOUDLY"

PAGE 35

PAGE 45 (3)   PAGE 63

PAGE 49

"BANDS BELIEVERS" - EMAIL

"THE END OF MKTNG AS WE KNOW IT"

"DESTINATION" PAGE 68

ZYMAN

AWARENESS VS
REASON TO BUY

CONSULTING (?) - ZGROUP; YOYODYNE
                            P 85
PAGE 78   (YAHOO)

"PERMISSION MKTNG" - GODIN

"SPIRAL MKTNG" - BERST

"CREATE + WIN" - KOTLER

"MARKETING"

THE LEADER'S EDGE

HOW TO THINK LIKE
THE WORLD'S GREATEST MARKETING MINDS

MARCIA LAYTON TURNER

MᴄGʀᴀᴡ-Hɪʟʟ

NEW YORK   SAN FRANCISCO   WASHINGTON, D.C.   AUCKLAND   BOGOTÁ
CARACAS   LISBON   LONDON   MADRID   MEXICO CITY   MILAN
MONTREAL   NEW DELHI   SAN JUAN   SINGAPORE
SYDNEY   TOKYO   TORONTO

Library of Congress Cataloging-in-Publication Data

Turner, Marcia Layton.
    How to think like the world's greatest marketing minds / Marcia Layton
Turner.
        p. cm.
    Includes index.
    ISBN 0-07-136070-0 (cloth)
    1. Marketing. 2. Marketing executives—United States   3. Business-
people—United States. I. Title.

HF5415.T774   2000
658.8–dc21   00-060924
                                                                CIP

McGraw-Hill

A Division of The McGraw-Hill Companies

1 2 3 4 5 6 7 8 9 0   DOC/DOC   0 6 5 4 3 2 1 0

ISBN 0-07-136070-0

This publication is designed to provide accurate and authoritative information in regard to the subject matter covered. It is sold with the understanding
that the publisher is not engaged in rendering legal, accounting, or other
professional service. If legal advice or other expert assistance is required, the
services of a competent professional person should be sought.
                    —From a declaration of principles jointly adopted by a committee of
                        the American Bar Association and a committee of publishers.

Book design by Michael Mendelsohn at MM Design 2000, Inc.
Printed and bound by R. R. Donnelley & Sons Company.

McGraw-Hill books are available at special quantity discounts to use as
premiums and sales promotions, or for use in corporate training programs.
For more information, please write to the Director of Special Sales, McGraw-Hill,
2 Penn Plaza, New York, NY 10121-2298. Or contact your local bookstore.

 This book is printed on recycled, acid-free paper
containing a minimum of 50% recycled, de-inked fiber.

To my wonderful husband, Charlie

CONTENTS

PREFACE

Marketing is such an incredibly hot topic today because well-thought-out marketing strategies and tactics can take a company's sale into the stratosphere—and the smart marketer right on up there with them. Marketing can cause careers to skyrocket, products to become best-sellers, and profits to rise exponentially.

Unfortunately, done poorly, it can also do the reverse, causing managers to be fired, companies to file for bankruptcy, and products to be shelved. What's the difference? Frequently, the decisions made regarding how a product or company is marketed make the biggest difference.

So how does one develop marketing strategies that work? Typically, smart companies look to other successful companies as models. By studying their strategies, their moves, and their decisions, other companies can mimic the winners' behavior and learn from their mistakes without suffering the consequences of those learning experiences.

That's exactly what this book is about. It's about showing you how leading marketers—some of the smartest marketing minds in the world—have faced and dealt with business situations. By studying how these marketers overcame challenges, took advantage of business opportunities, and built multimillion-dollar empires, you can model their success.

It's unlikely that you'll want to apply each and every strategy any one marketing leader has used, but by mixing and matching some of the best of several marketers, you can compile your own unique approach, based on what's worked before in other industries. In this book, we present the marketing strategies of 11 marketing leaders whom we think you should know about.

WHAT MAKES THEM MARKETING LEADERS

What makes these individuals leaders and gurus in their own right is their history of success. Granted, there are many others who may have had just as much success who could have qualified for inclusion in the book. But the group profiled here had a combination of smarts and intuition that resulted in their success. It wasn't outside resources or help that propelled them, as is the case with many other successful marketers: It was their business savvy and drive. The following are some of the things they all have in common.

GOAL SETTING

Each of the leaders had clearly defined goals. For example, Martha Stewart, wanted to be the next Julia Child, Phil Knight's mission was to build a company to defeat Adidas, and Sergio Zyman's eye was on increasing worldwide consumption of Coca-Cola.

But what is also true is that those early goals gave way to even larger objectives. Seth Godin's initial foray into permission marketing happened more than a decade ago when he was a consultant to Prodigy and later developed into a whole marketing movement that has changed the way Internet promotions occur. Jay Conrad Levinson's guerrilla marketing concept has become the rallying cry of small businesses everywhere, and instead of writing *one* best-selling book, Levinson has a whole series.

What makes these marketers so remarkable is, in many cases, the way in which they have successfully applied various marketing concepts. Taking approaches that have worked in one industry and applying it to their own is one smart move that many have made, as is perfecting a tried-and-true tactic for their own purposes.

A LITTLE LUCK

But, truth be told, each has also had his or her share of luck. Take Phil Knight and his phenomenal Nike shoes. Sales of his innovative sneakers took off in part because of their unusual features, but the fitness craze that was taking off played an important role as well. Without the jogging trend, Nike may never have gotten off the ground.

Likewise, Martha Stewart would probably never have achieved her goal of having her own television show, like Julia Child, had she not been featured in a national article in *People* magazine. That visibility opened up doors and began to establish her as the reigning diva of domesticity.

TEAMWORK

Collaboration is also a common theme, with customers, suppliers, and even competitors being brought in as partners to help a company achieve a goal. And these smart marketers know it—they recognize that it would be futile to try and achieve on their own what they've done through teamwork. Seth Godin, for example, brought together Internet technology and Fortune 500 companies that were looking for a way to break through the clutter. And it worked.

Consumers were also important collaborators. Many consultants advise turning to customers for feedback regarding new-product development—especially in the high-tech world, says Geoffrey Moore. Sometimes, customers have a better handle on what the market is looking for than the companies developing the products, which is why outside input can be critical.

HOW CAN YOU DUPLICATE THEIR LEVEL OF SUCCESS?

Is there a way of duplicating the successful marketer's level of success? The truth is you can't. Each marketing superstar profiled here achieved an amazing level of success because of a unique combination of circumstances that he or she encountered. Some, like Phil Knight and Martha Stewart, hit on an idea just at the beginning of a shift in the community's lifestyle that significantly increased their odds of success from the start. Others, such as Geoffrey Moore, studied a particular phenomenon to better understand it and to provide guidance in how to deal with it.

Still others were superior at responding to consumer demands. Herb Kelleher of Southwest Airlines heard passengers' cries for better treatment and lower fares, and Sergio Zyman boosted sales of Coca-Cola during his tenure by recognizing and understanding the consumer's unique bond with the brand. Consultant Seth Godin developed a way to calm consumer fears about privacy issues and irritation over junk email and Jay Conrad Levinson came up with a host of marketing tactics that were just perfect for a company with a small budget.

Professor Phil Kotler and consultants Don Peppers and Martha Rogers, PhD, practically invented new theories and approaches to marketing, Kotler with his marketing management strategies and Pepper and Rogers with one-to-one marketing, their replacement for mass marketing. And consultant, adviser, and guru Regis McKenna pointed out the astounding fact that, sometimes, providing better customer service means enabling customers to do it themselves.

Madonna, with her innovative, always changing persona, is so unique, that you'd be a fool to try and duplicate her rise to fame and fortune.

What you *can* do is study the steps each one took, in light of external forces such as shifts in lifestyle and purchasing trends, and apply those that fit your company's particular situation.

Take the deliberate strategies each employed and adapt it to your own situation. There are many winning ideas here that have been tried only in a limited number of situations. Perhaps one will be your ticket to stardom.

ACKNOWLEDGMENTS

Several people have made this project a joy to work on, and I am honored to have been associated with them: first, my editor, the supportive and creative Mary Glenn at McGraw-Hill. A close second was my agent, Lisa Swayne of The Swayne Agency, who provided insight and recommendations that significantly improved the final product; just as important were my rough-draft editor and close friend, Audrey Seybold, who always seemed to find the time to review chapters and offer great suggestions despite her own breakneck schedule, and, Paul Hudson of Roberts Communications, who kindly read through some of my writing and offered suggestions that were gratefully incorporated.

Although I didn't always have the chance to speak directly with the marketing gurus featured in this book, I thank them for their own unique applications of the tools that marketing offers. Every one of them has had an important impact on the field, helping to enhance the prestige associated with being a marketing professional.

Part One

GURU
DOERS

UNCONVENTIONAL ANTICS BUILD A LEADING AIRLINE

Herb Kelleher

We've always done it differently. You know, we don't assign seats. Used to be we only had about four people on the whole plane, so the idea of assigned seats just made people laugh. Now the reason is you can turn the airplanes quicker at the gate. And if you can turn an airplane quicker, you can have it fly more routes each day. That generates more revenue, so you can offer lower fares.

—Herb Kelleher,
CEO, Southwest Airlines

3

INTRODUCTION

One of Southwest Airlines' ads several years ago conveys the style and personality of the nation's most unconventional airline. It was a full-page ad in the *Wall Street Journal* responding to Northwest Airlines' claim of being number one in customer satisfaction. Southwest's response? "Liar, liar, pants on fire."

In an industry of cookie-cutter competitors, all providing remarkably similar services, Herb Kelleher, chairman, president, and CEO of Southwest, has placed the airline in a class of its own by striving to give customers exactly what they want in air travel. "They want to get there safely, on time, and with pleasant people," he claims. And that understanding drives how Southwest does business.

Kelleher's management style, which epitomizes the company's marketing image of low-cost fun travel, has led Southwest to transform the airline industry. The company has made air travel affordable for a whole new segment of the market, even turning some—formerly nonflying—customers into frequent flyers.

Although just a small regional airline at its founding in 1971, Southwest is now the fourth-largest U.S. carrier, with an astounding record of profitability—27 straight years—that has earned national recognition for the company's superior customer service. The airline now boasts sales of more than $4.7 billion and has more than 29,000 employees.

In 1997, Southwest earned the U.S. government's "Triple Crown" for best baggage handling, best on-time performance, and fewest customer complaints of any major airline for the fifth consecutive year. And additional awards have followed, including a *Computerworld*/Smithsonian Award for outstanding use of technology, *Chief Executive* magazine's 1999 Chief Executive of the Year, and *Fortune's* most admired airline and best place to work in the United States.

THE EARLY YEARS

Southwest Airlines was an idea conceived by Texas entrepreneur Rollin King and his banker, John Parker, in 1966. At the time, King owned a small commuter air service operating out of San Antonio. Parker suggested to King that he start an intrastate airline to operate between Houston, Dallas, and San Antonio, "the Golden Triangle of Texas," because of the exorbitant fares the major airlines were charging to fly between those cities.

King looked into it and found that the idea had merit: All three cities were experiencing strong economic growth and were far enough apart to make driving inconvenient. He also studied airlines with similar business models, such as *Pacific Southwest Airline* (PSA) in California, which operated between economically healthy cities that were too far apart to drive between. PSA had proven that the concept could work.

Kelleher originally became part of the Southwest organization as its legal counsel. He had graduated in 1956 from NYU law school, clerked for a New Jersey supreme court justice, and joined a Newark, New Jersey, law firm before deciding to relocate to Texas, his wife's home state. Rollin King hired Kelleher to handle the legal aspects of getting approval for the new airline. Throughout the next five years, as numerous battles were fought—all the way to the U.S. Supreme Court—Kelleher became more and more personally invested in getting the airline off the ground.

Kelleher became chairman of Southwest in 1978, following the leadership of Lamar Muse, a flamboyant marketer and financier who was responsible for infusing the company with its unique corporate culture. Under Muse's tenure, employees were taught that it was OK to be outrageous, as long as the behavior benefited Southwest's customers. He also infused the organization with a focus on profitability. Much of the company's emphasis on speed and productivity is a result of Muse's early challenges to the employees.

Kelleher has taken the strong foundation laid by Muse one step further. Giving employees the responsibility, authority, and incentive to do whatever it takes to satisfy customer needs has proven to be a magical formula: Southwest was one of the first airlines to institute a profit-sharing program that benefits all employees. But over time, as the airline has grown and flourished, one thing Southwest has not done is grow beyond its capabilities. Kelleher is one of the few corporate leaders to keep his organization keenly focused on doing what it does best—short-haul flying at a low price. Continued profitability, rather than growth for growth's sake, is always the goal.

THE SOUTHWEST AIRLINES BUSINESS MODEL

From its inception, Southwest has focused on direct short-haul routes instead of following the traditional hub-and-

No FRILLS + No HUBS = LOW COST

spoke strategy used by the major carriers. This decision is at the crux of the company's marketing superiority.

By shuttling between smaller cities, such as Manchester, New Hampshire, and Albany, New York, Southwest eliminates the higher costs associated with hub routes. Since airlines make money only when planes are flying, the less time planes spend on the ground, the more profitable the company is. Hub-and-spoke systems are less profitable because they require the airplanes to stay on the ground significantly longer to await connecting flights. Eschewing the hub-and-spoke strategy enables Southwest to keep its planes airborne 11.5 hours a day, versus just 8.6 for other carriers.

More importantly for Southwest, higher costs defeat the company's mission: being as profitable as possible to ensure job security for its employees and to make air travel affordable for more people.

Positioning itself as a low-cost carrier, Southwest endears itself to passengers who would just as well not pay for "extras" like fancy meals. Instead, passengers are treated to bags of peanuts—an estimated 60 million bags a year!—at an average cost of 20 cents per passenger, compared with $5 for the big guys' meals.

Southwest's average trip length is 441 miles, with an average one-way airfare of $78. Eliminating more involved services, such as prepared meals and assigned seating, also helps Southwest turn its planes around faster. As a result, Southwest has achieved the lowest cost per available seat mile for equivalent trips. To its credit, the company cancels fewer flights than any other airline and has one of the best on-time arrival records.

What Southwest has done perhaps better than any other airline is stay focused on its mission. Its goal of providing low-cost, shorter flights has never wavered. And that fact is another reason that the company has performed so well.

STICK TO YOUR NICHE

Although Southwest is the fourth-largest airline in the United States, its innovative and brash business tactics have made it the airline the top three try to emulate. When Southwest proved that it could actually make money charging rock-bottom fares, major airlines rushed to lower their fares. Early on, Southwest demonstrated that it was willing to fight for its survival, trying tactics thought unworkable in the airline business. For example, it refused to move its operations from a smaller Houston airport to a higher cost major airport when the larger airport opened, causing other airlines to attempt to force Southwest to relocate with them. But Southwest would have none of it and won the right to stay put.

Repeatedly, other airlines have changed their business tactics in order to try to compete with Southwest. And they have learned that it is virtually impossible to do so.

After defining its service as short-haul only, Southwest broke new ground in creating a whole new class of customers: those who would have traveled by other means had the airfare been more expensive. As the Freibergs report in *NUTS!*, major airlines had previously segmented the market into two groups: those who could afford to fly and those who couldn't. Their focus was squarely on those passengers who could afford to fly. Southwest, on the other hand, decided to try to make it affordable for everyone to fly, thereby increasing the potential market severalfold.

Not content to stop at that, Southwest took its strategy one step further and revolutionized the airline pricing model. Although two-tiered pricing had been used to a small extent, Southwest decided to follow the laws of supply and demand and make it more expensive for people to fly during peak times and less expensive during off-peak hours. Such an approach is now used industrywide as a way to efficiently fill planes.

Although other airlines mimic Southwest's strategy, the company has stayed true to its niche. Southwest refused to buy larger planes, enter larger markets, and raise ticket prices—even as little as $2 to $3. As a result of this smart move, the company continues to operate at a profit while other airlines go bankrupt.

THINK SMALL

Like Seth Godin, who expounds on the advantages small companies have when it comes to flexibility in the market-place, Kelleher strives to hold onto Southwest's small-company roots. By continuing to think and act like a small company, the airline is more willing to take risks, do the unthinkable, and achieve extraordinary growth in one of the most competitive markets in existence. In an interview in *Fortune*, Kelleher says that he tells his employees, "Think small and act small, and we'll get bigger. Think big, be complacent, be cocky, and we'll get smaller."

By retaining the underdog spirit, Southwest has led the way with creative solutions to challenges posed by the competition. Frequently, the innovations have involved better use of technology, helping the company retain its lowest-cost structure.

One such innovation, which reflects the company's agility and flexibility, was "ticketless travel." Now an industry standard, ticketless travel was initiated in 1994, when Southwest was kicked off of the main airline reservation system by United, Continental, and Delta for introducing lower-cost, short-run services in markets they served. Consequently, travel agents could no longer automatically generate Southwest tickets and would have had to write them up for customers manually. Since the airline knew that requiring such additional work would significantly cut into its sales, the ticketless concept and system was developed in record time: four months.

Southwest's solution was to encourage customers to deal directly with the airline personnel, who would issue a confirmation number that could be presented at the airport before flight departure. Ticketless travel also made online reservations possible.

Perhaps because of its ticketless travel innovation, Southwest was the first airline to launch a Web site (www.southwest.com), designed internally by ambitious employees. The design of the site attempts to reflect the homey appeal of the airline's personality, while building in state-of-the-art capabilities to make reservations simpler for customers. *Transport World* recently honored the site as the best in the industry.

Another innovation is NewRes, Southwest's totally new airline reservation system. Introducing its own system has enabled the company to be less reliant on other host systems, which had put Southwest at a disadvantage for bookings. Now Southwest can be more flexible in its pricing, marketing, seating, *and* booking.

A NEED FOR SPEED

Gate turnaround times of 10 minutes were unheard of when Southwest set the new standard for its gate employees. The move was made solely to enable the company to operate with one less plane during a time of financial crisis in the early 1970s. Cutting the turnaround time saved the company an estimated 25 percent of its operating expenses. Even today, the company turns its planes around in less than 20 minutes, which is approximately half the industry average.

Aircraft turns of 15 and 20 minutes also reduce the number of planes the company needs to operate—approximately 35 fewer than an airline with 40- to 55-minute turns. Those savings, which are more than $1 billion, based on the cost of a new Boeing 737, are part of what makes it possible for Southwest to continue to offer such low fares.

Providing a continental breakfast for its passengers in the gate area, instead of on the plane, is another way that Southwest keeps its planes in the air a larger percentage of the time. Instead of having to spend time cleaning up a plane, airport crews can take responsibility for cleaning up the gate area once the plane has taken off. Time savings = lower cost = higher profits for the company, not to mention the notoriety of doing things differently than every other airline.

In a number of instances throughout its history, Southwest has demonstrated its ability to move swiftly to take advantage of opportunities. In several cases in which the airline was maneuvering to take over the space other airlines were giving up, it moved quickly to build new check-in counters or put up walls in order to be able to start flying in and out of the airport at the first possible moment. Southwest doesn't waste time!

KEEP IT SIMPLE

Kelleher's effort to keep operations simple is reflected in a number of business strategies, with standardization being the major one. Owning and operating only one type of airplane—the Boeing 737—keeps maintenance, training, and parts inventory to a minimum. Southwest has standardized its computer equipment for the same reasons, thus saving money as well as time by keeping operations simpler.

Requiring that pilots be certified as captains is another way that Southwest keeps things simple and, at the same time, builds flexibility and agility into its workforce. With every pilot being qualified to serve as captain, Southwest has achieved a built-in level of cross-training. Flight crews can be easily reassigned without having to factor in varying levels of training or qualifications.

Boarding passes are another area where simpler is better. Southwest has shunned the industry standard multi-part boarding passes in favor of simple, reusable plastic ones. Not only do they speed the boarding process by eliminating much of the unnecessary information that appears on typical passes, but also they save money.

"EMPLOYEES COME FIRST"

The key to Southwest Airlines' success, claims Kelleher, is its people—all 29,000 of them. Southwest is meticulous about hiring people with the right attitude, which he defines as humility, modesty, and altruism. But humor is also an essential ingredient at a company that encourages its employees to dress up on holidays, sing airline safety precautions, and play practical jokes on passengers. Kelleher explains that Southwest hires people with the right attitude and then trains them for the specific role they are needed to fill, unlike other companies that look first and foremost for experience.

The Southwest corporate culture is a clear competitive advantage—the "intangibles" Kelleher calls it—that distinguishes the airline from its larger competitors. Although the bigger airlines can buy the same planes, as well as invest in the same baggage-handling equipment or ticket counters, Kelleher notes, it's very difficult to imitate the Southwest attitude. "The way you treat your employees is the way they will treat your customers," says Kelleher, stressing the importance of making employees feel valued.

That culture was probably born in the earliest days of the airline's existence, says Kelleher, when the major airlines did everything they could think of to put Southwest out of business. At that time, with four airplanes and 70 employees, it was essential that each individual contribute 100 percent, or the company would have folded. A "survivalist mentality" evolved—"one for all or all for one, or together we perish"—that continues to affect how the company is operated.

The company values that have evolved reflect the spirit and priorities of Southwest. Like its core mission, which is to stay profitable, the company's core values speak volumes about its corporate culture. The authors of *NUTS!* identified 13 major values that they maintain are part of the Southwest culture:

- Profitability
- Low cost
- Family
- Fun
- Love
- Hard work
- Individuality
- Ownership
- Legendary service
- Egalitarianism
- Common sense
- Simplicity
- Altruism

Interestingly just two of the 13 values—low cost and profitability— are economic values, which shows that a company need not be solely financially driven to succeed. A focus on how people are treated is equally important.

So it should be no surprise that, unlike other airlines, Southwest is unionized and happy about it. Eighty-seven percent union, to be exact. Perhaps Kelleher's attitude toward labor negotiations is a sign of why union and nonunion workers collaborate so well: He asks himself "What's the most we can give without jeopardizing job security and profitability?" And in situations where he needs to ask for pay freezes or cuts, he has been known to offer to freeze his own pay and bonuses during the same period.

INTERNAL BRANDING IS AS IMPORTANT AS EXTERNAL BRANDING

The word *branding* is typically used to describe the process of marketing a company's products or services to its target audience by identifying certain features or benefits the company offers. Typically, branding and marketing are outwardly focused—concerned primarily with building long-term customer relationships that will lead to sales.

But for Southwest, having its employees understand and internalize the company's mission has been even more important. Part of that process of "internal branding" has been working to achieve employee satisfaction, so that the workers, in turn, can communicate that level of satisfaction to the company's customers.

Where other companies cite customer or shareholder satisfaction as their mission, Southwest focuses on employee satisfaction. Kelleher's reasoning, in a 1999 interview in *Chief Executive*, is that "If your employees are satisfied and happy and dedicated and inspired by what they're doing, then they make your customers happy and they come back and that makes your shareholders happy." By concentrating on its employees, Southwest markets first to its *internal* audience, which can then share the brand's promise with customers.

Kelleher's belief that "Profit is a by-product of customer service" has been borne out by recent Harvard Business School research showing a solid link between employee satisfaction, customer satisfaction, and profitability—in that order.

Some of the steps Southwest takes to enhance employee satisfaction involve frequent communication. Kelleher himself, with the help of his second in command, Colleen Barrett, executive vice president for customers, sends out birthday cards to each employee every year, as well as notes of congratulations on weddings and new babies, and condolences when appropriate. He also keeps employees updated on his activities through a column called "So What Was Herb Doing All This Time?" in the company's *Luv Lines* newsletter. And some of the time, he actually helps his team out by pitching in on the job. He's been known to haul luggage with the baggage handlers and assist crews during flights.

Celebrations are also a big part of the Southwest culture. Parties help employees get to know each other, as well as reinforce the company's emphasis on fun. In the hallways of Southwest headquarters, more than 1500 images of employees are displayed, showing the workers engaged in activities ranging from partying to receiving awards. In everything the airline does, it is evident that the company recognizes that its employees truly are the key to its success.

While employees at other companies may not even recognize their CEO, Southwest employees receive some kind of communication from Kelleher an average of five times per year.

BE OUTRAGEOUS

The media have played an important role in the success of Southwest Airlines, providing the company with millions of dollars of free exposure. And all Southwest had to do was to be consistently newsworthy, which has been relatively easy to do with its ongoing outrageous antics.

Back in 1971, Southwest's battle to receive approval to operate was reported as a David-and-Goliath type story in Texas, immediately positioning the fledgling airline as the worthy underdog. Such an image has pervaded the company's culture and stayed with the organization for decades. It also helped spawn word-of-mouth advertising, a crucial marketing method the company has relied on for much of its growth. As Shelly Phelps, a former secretary, explains in *NUTS!*, when half of the company's first-year $700,000 advertising budget was spent in the first month of operation, it became clear that Southwest was going to have to use other means of promoting itself. Word-of-mouth advertising was one of the few options the company could afford; it was just a matter of finding low-cost ways to encourage people to talk about it. "For the talk value," she says, "we decided that we needed to make our company absolutely outrageous."

Through the years, being outrageous has run the gamut from the company dress code (flight attendants on Southwest wore hot pants in the early days), to painting the planes unusual colors and themes (such as the killer whale plane, "Shamu One," so decorated in honor of Southwest's initial sponsorship of Sea World of Texas), to dress-up days on holidays (for example, Kelleher has arrived at events in Elvis garb).

Communicating the personality of Southwest has been the objective of the company's promotional efforts, whether through press releases or paid ads. Frequently using a form of storytelling, Southwest lets its customers and employees speak out about what makes it different. Getting across what makes Southwest special is the challenge of all marketing communications activities, as well as a way of enticing customers to experience the airline's unconventional attitude. And humor is the common thread.

Whether poking fun at itself or at the competition, Southwest consistently incorporates a humorous angle in its advertising. While humor has long been known to be an effective marketing tool, the extent to which Southwest incorporates it is unparalleled.

MAKE EMPLOYEES PART OWNERS

In addition to receiving generous compensation packages, Southwest employees are also privy to a top-notch profit-sharing package that includes stock ownership; together they now own approximately 11 percent of the company. But more important than the financial benefits is the mindset that business ownership provides.

As part owners of Southwest, its employees are more willing to pitch in and do whatever is necessary to keep the business operating and profitable. With a vested interest in the performance of the company, employees are frequently more willing to go above and beyond the call of duty to improve the company. With ownership also comes a sense of pride that is communicated to customers in every interaction.

Tammy Romo, director of investor relations at Southwest, says in *NUTS!*, "Profit-sharing aligns the employee's interests with the interests of the company. Our people are more conscious about protecting the company's assets and accomplishing its goals because their well-being is tied to the company's well-being."

THE FUTURE OF SOUTHWEST

Southwest's low fares and high marks for customer service have made it an extremely desirable airline—one that many cities would love to have as a carrier. As a result, airports nationwide have begun to try and woo Southwest to them. But with Southwest entering just one or two cities a year—with no plans to increase that expansion rate—the competition is fierce.

When Allentown, Pennsylvania, learned that its Lehigh Valley International Airport would not be one of the airline's newest markets, the staff sent a box of Grinch dolls to Southwest in jest. The joke backfired, however, and Lehigh Valley received a spirited rhyme, along with a copy of Dr. Seuss's *Green Eggs and Ham*:

> We will not go from here to there
> We would not go there on a dare
> We will not go there on a boat
> We would not go there with a goat.
> We would not go there if we drove trains
> You will not get our Air-O-Planes
> You will not see us in your air
> You will not get our great low fare.

Obviously, Southwest has no intention of toning down its humorous corporate personality, thank goodness. So we can expect to see the company continue to grow and achieve more and more success.

KELLEHER MARKETING MANIFESTO

Stick to your niche.

Think small.

A need for speed.

Keep it simple.

"Employees come first."

Be outrageous.

Make employees part owners.

REFERENCES

"Aim low, lefty, they're ridin' Shetlands!" by Cliff McGoon, *Communication World*, April–May 1999, p. 30.

"Air herb's secret weapon," by J. P. Donlon, *Chief Executive*, July–August 1999, p.32.

"The fly boys," *Fortune*, May 24, 1999, p. 238.

"Have fun, make money," by Stephanie Gruner, *Inc.*, May 1998, p. 123.

"How herb keeps Southwest hopping," *Money*, June 1, 1999, p. 61.

"The Jack and Herb show," *Fortune*, January 11, 1999, p. 32.

"Management ideas through time," *Management Review*, January 1998, p. 16.

Nuts! Southwest Airlines' Crazy Recipe for Business and Personal Success, by Kevin and Jackie Freiberg, Broadway Books, 1996.

"Out of the office…and into the trenches," by Peter Nauert, *Chief Executive*, June 1998, p. 48.

"Reflecting on peanuts, profits and medical practices," by Neil Baum, *American Medical News*, June 9, 1997, p. 18.

"Sky king," by Kathleen Melymuka, *Computerworld*, September 28, 1998, p. 68.

"So much work, so little time," by Shelly Branch, *Fortune*, February 2, 1997, p. 115.

CHAPTER TWO

THE MAN BEHIND THE SWOOSH

Philip Knight

Michael Jordan is not the most incredible, the most colorful, the most amazing, the most flashy, or the most mind-boggling thing in the NBA. His shoes are.

—*Chicago Journal* sports writer
Steve Aschberner (in *Swoosh*)

INTRODUCTION

Who ever convinced us that we needed different shoes for different sports activities? I mean, how different can athletic shoes really be? Apparently very different, if we are to believe Philip Hampson Knight, CEO and cofounder of Nike, the country's leading athletic shoe manufacturer.

Because of Knight's ingenuity and marketing savvy, we now have the ability to choose from among hundreds of styles and designs when buying sneakers. There's a sneaker for basketball, a sneaker for running, a sneaker for bowling, one for tennis, another for aerobics, and on and on, some at prices of more than $100 per pair. This, despite the fact that, according to *Brandweek*, 8 out of 10 pairs of athletic shoes aren't even purchased for sports.

But we have been convinced, in part by Nike, that we need the latest-and-greatest sports shoe in order to perform well. This demand has fed Nike's growth for several decades, making it the marketing powerhouse that it is today.

Surprisingly, there were just a handful of sneaker styles for all activities before Nike entered the game in the early 1970s—before shoes became a major fashion statement and one of the trendiest products around. By 1987, there were 487 separate footwear brands, where there had been fewer than a dozen at Nike's start.

By recruiting some of the world's best-known and well-liked professional athletes to represent the company, and by investing smartly in promotions, Nike became a household name, capturing the lion's share of the athletic-shoe market.

Although growth has slowed somewhat in recent years, Nike remains the industry leader, poised to reenergize its brand with a continuous introduction of new products.

THE GENESIS OF NIKE

Before Nike, there was Tiger, a Japanese running shoe manufactured by Onitsuka and imported by a small Beaverton, Oregon-based sporting goods company named *Blue Ribbon Sports* (BRS). BRS's owner, Phil Knight, dreamt of building a running-shoe giant that would eclipse then-market leader Adidas, and Onitsuka's Tiger shoe was his starting point. At the time, the Tiger shoe was one of the lightest and fastest shoes on the market, and very popular with student athletes, Knight's target market.

Sales of the Tiger established BRS as a credible company and helped to build relationships with college-level track-and-field coaches, as well as prominent retailers, nationwide.

While Knight is the name most commonly associated with Nike, he alone didn't start the company. His partner and cofounder, Bill Bowerman, was the actual brains behind the revolutionary designs Nike was later known for. Both Bowerman and Knight invested $500 in the late 1960s to establish their new company, selling Tigers out of the trunk of Bowerman's car.

But Tigers would later be dropped by BRS, primarily because of confusion over the company's territorial rights. Knight knew that a totally new brand would have to be created in order for the company to survive. And Bowerman came through with a revolutionary design

originally pieced together to help his track team improve
its performance.

Bowerman, then a University of Oregon track coach,
developed a new class of shoe—waffle soled—with the help
of his wife's waffle iron, latex, leather, and glue. Those shoes
would later become the basis for Nike's business and the
start of a history of innovations that Nike would try to hold
on to for years.

The Nike moniker was introduced in 1971, and a new
era began. Nike, the Greek goddess of victory, seemed a fit-
ting name for a company dedicated to helping its customers compete and win. A rough logo was created that
resembled a check mark, later to be referred to as the
"Swoosh."

But Nike's first shoe was not a running shoe: It was a
football shoe. The decision to manufacture and market a
football shoe was Nike's way of striking out on its own
while still bound by noncompete arrangements with Onitsuka. Since Onitsuka did not have a football shoe, Knight
felt that he could successfully argue, if necessary, that Nike
was not competing with Onitsuka at all.

Unfortunately, that first shoe did not perform as Knight
had hoped. Built in Mexico, the shoe was not tested to perform in cold, snowy conditions on the football field and
ended up disintegrating. Nike quickly gained a reputation
as a cheap shoe. Over time, the company would overcome
that disastrous beginning, becoming known for quality and
creative designs.

By 1980, half of all the running shoes sold in the United
States were Nikes, featuring the now-famous Swoosh symbol, and by 1982, Nike was the dominant athletic-shoe
company in the nation. After a rough patch in the late
1980s, Nike rebounded with its "Just Do It" advertising
campaign and reclaimed the number-one slot by the early
1990s. A short slide in the late 1990s due to a financial cri-

sis in Asia caused layoffs at Nike, but by 1999, profits increased at a double-digit pace, and the company appeared back on track.

Although Bowerman died in late 1999, to Nike employees his waffle iron will always symbolize the company's innovative thinking and design capabilities.

SNEAKY GENIUS—NEW-PRODUCT INNOVATIONS

Sneakers were sneakers until Nike came along. What differentiated Nike at the start was its unusual design. Waffle-soled shoes had never been tried before Bowerman's crude experiments. But that experiment was perfected and later spawned many new shoe designs. The "dipped backtab," designed to reduce pressure on the Achilles tendon, was a Nike innovation, as was the square cleat.

The design team's willingness to combine pieces from various different types of footwear was what made Nikes so different. A sandal bottom was the base of one of Nike's designs, for example, because of its comfort.

But Nike's focus on the sole of the shoe as the source of improvement ultimately generated several cutting-edge designs that would later be copied by competitors. The air-cushioned heel, gel pads, and lights were all Nike inventions, creating new demand for its shoes with each new product introduced. Runners and then athletes of numerous sports turned to Nike for state-of-the-art athletic footwear that would give them the edge in competition.

Subbrands were also created for each celebrity athlete representing Nike, playing off of the appeal of each individual and his or her sport. In some cases, the Swoosh was made less evident; in others, a totally new symbol represented the new brand. The Air Jordan shoe, for example, was created for Michael Jordan, while a cross-training shoe was developed for two-sport athlete Bo Jackson, and an entire golf shoe and apparel line was designed for Tiger Woods. The combined appeal of the Nike brand and sports stars has resulted in millions of sales dollars over the years.

While Nike has always invested heavily in *research and development* (R&D), its newest product, the Alpha line, is the result of a tripled R&D budget since 1995. Alpha will be positioned as a holistic approach to outfitting the athlete—from shoe to apparel to equipment—and is anticipated to once again drive consumers to retailers in droves.

INVEST IN MARKETING

In addition to spending heavily on celebrity endorsements and donating products to amateur athletes, Nike has always been smart about its investment in marketing and promotional activities. Where the average U.S. corporation spends 4 percent of its gross sales on marketing, Nike spends multiples of that. In 1997, the company's marketing budget was $978 million, on sales of roughly $9 billion. The size of this investment is perhaps one reason that Nike's Swoosh logo seems ubiquitous—it is!

Although the company has perhaps the largest marketing budget of its industry, that was not always the case. Throughout its history, Nike has relied much more on promotions than on paid advertising to reach out to customers—mainly because that was all the company could afford.

Providing products to athletes and signing endorsement deals was a big part of Nike's promotional efforts, but sponsoring road races and creating track clubs were equally important. One of the biggest successes was the Athletics West running club, based in Eugene, Oregon, in the late

1970s. The club's purpose was to subsidize training and sponsor races for a group of athletes, without overtly pushing the Nike name. Athletes were provided Nike gear that would be seen during races and competitions, giving the company the promotional plug it was looking for. But leaving references to Nike out of the club's name was one of the smartest moves the firm made. By distancing the Nike name from the club, the company avoided turning the group into an obvious commercial enterprise. Nike officials referred to this strategy as "whispering loudly"—allowing the consumer to figure things out for him- or herself. Athletics West became the model that competitors attempted to copy, but never could successfully.

ALIGN YOURSELF WITH IMAGE LEADERS

Nike's strategy of paying sports celebrities to wear its shoes was brilliant, and a major reason that the company has grown so much, so quickly. Knight believed that "if he could get a few 'cool guys' to use his products, then his business would be a success," a recent *Accountancy* article reported.

From the beginning, the company signed endorsement deals with leading athletes in a variety of sports, with tennis, basketball, and running being the strong suits. Having strong performers wearing its shoes helped to position Nike as a company of fellow athletes who understood the challenges faced by their customers.

Nike also gave the best athletes an incentive to wear its shoes: a percentage of shoe sales. The revolutionary Nike Pro Club was a group of elite basketball players handpicked by the company, who were guaranteed a share of royalties on sales of basketball shoes. The first year of the program,

1975, each of 10 players had a two-year, $2000-minimum contract. And at the end of the year, with basketball-shoe sales having quadrupled, they each received more than $8000—much more than the minimum that had been set.

Although Nike invested heavily in endorsement deals with athletes, it wasn't until Michael Jordan came along in 1985 that the company hit the jackpot. Once Jordan became a Nike pitchman, the company supported its multimillion-dollar investment—its largest ever in one athlete—with a huge television advertising campaign directed by Spike Lee. Nike commercials led the way in linking basketball, fashion, and celebrity personalities. And the result was a huge surge in demand for its basketball footwear.

With Jordan, Nike took the never-before tack of introducing a line of Michael Jordan shoes and apparel, complete with its own logo. Air Jordan shoes brought in $100 million in sales the first year.

Following Michael Jordan as Nike endorser was football and baseball star Bo Jackson, who helped increase demand for Nike's cross-training shoe. The "Bo knows..." series of commercials sparked yet another jump in demand for the company's shoes.

Years later, golf phenomenon Tiger Woods was signed on as the newest Nike celebrity, getting $90 million for a multiyear contract. With Woods just 24, Nike is betting that its investment will pay off. But given Woods's record so far, and his personableness, it's likely that Nike will get its money's worth.

DONATE A PRODUCT TO ESTABLISH CONSUMER PREFERENCE

Just as Microsoft gives away its Internet Explorer free as part of new computer purchases, to establish a preference for the product, Nike has long given away sports gear to high school and college teams. While part of the reason for this support hearkens back to the company's history of working to improve the performance of the athletes, its motives are not all pure.

Nike marketers have long recognized the value of having top high school and college athletes and coaches sporting the firm's clothing and footwear. In some cases, having the Nike Swoosh appear on a college athlete may be just as advantageous as seeing the same equipment on a professional.

Because amateur athletes are not permitted to accept gifts or money of any sort, Nike donates its equipment to the schools, coaches, and teams, associated with those athletes as part of the company's sponsorship of Olympic trials. And in return, Nike earns significant media coverage and the potential allegiance of the athletes who receive the shoes and outfits.

SECURE RETAIL COMMITMENTS

During Nike's fast-growth period in the mid-1970s, the company hit a cash crunch and was having difficulty managing deliveries of its products. Retailers threatened to drop the Nike product line if deliveries were not made on time. But without a realistic estimate of product demand, Nike would have to overproduce in order to assure that its customers' needs were met. And the company simply couldn't afford to take such a risk. So Nike developed an advance-commitment program that would help the company forecast sales more accurately, while securing an upfront purchase commitment.

Nike approached its largest customers and proposed its new Futures program. Customers received a 5 to 7 percent discount for any order that they placed several months in advance of delivery, and they also got a guarantee that they would receive at least 90 percent of that order on time. Knowing exactly how many shoes to order, what sizes, and what colors gave Nike a significant competitive advantage when it came to meeting customer delivery expectations and reduced the company's inventory-holding cost, since it didn't have to order more than what was needed.

OUTSOURCE PRODUCTION

Nike is viewed as a pioneer in production. Instead of trying to compete with its then-larger competitors, from the outset Nike designed its shoes in-house and outsourced virtually all of the manufacturing of its products to countries in Southeast Asia. Nike does not manufacture *any* of the shoes it sells—it relies on its subcontractors for 100 percent of its production.

Through outsourcing, the company significantly reduced its operating costs to the point where few other companies could surpass its profitability. Nike currently employs approximately 500,000 workers at 350 subcontractors in 35 countries. Most of the workers are in Vietnam, Thailand, Pakistan, and Indonesia. In fact, says Knight, Nike shoes make up 5 percent of all the exports coming out of Vietnam.

FACE NEGATIVE PRESS HEAD-ON

Unfortunately, Nike has had its share of negative press in recent years. Beginning with allegations of sweatshop labor overseas in the early 1990s, the shine has worn from Nike's well-heeled image. But the company has not been hurt nearly as much as it could have, primarily because it has dealt expertly with negative reports.

When accusations of unfair labor practices surfaced, Nike did exactly what it should have—become proactive. In responding immediately to the lukewarm commissioned report on its labor practices, the company took control of information dissemination. Next, Nike placed full-page ads in seven major newspapers, urging consumers to visit its Web site and call an 800 number to receive more information on the company's plan to address the deficiencies cited in the report.

By responding immediately with accurate and thoughtful information, Nike lessened the potential backlash from the public accusations and fended off the possibility of even more negative publicity it would have gotten by not responding. Remember the Tylenol tampering scare? In contrast to executives in that situation, Nike made all the right moves, which is why sales of its shoes are unlikely to be seriously affected in the long term.

GO WHERE THE MONEY IS: THE INTERNET

With consumer spending over the Internet growing by leaps and bounds, smart distributors and retailers have staked out their territory for the long haul. According to a *Knight-Ridder/Tribune Business News* article, although less than $200 million worth of sports shoes and apparel is sold online today (out of $77 billion sold in the United States overall), within the next five years the online figure could grow to $4 billion..

Nike has taken its time establishing a presence on the Web, creating a site that has won kudos from consumers and industry observers alike. *Advertising Age* hailed the site, proclaiming, "Nike is an example of how to put together an integrated marketing campaign with the TV and Internet playing to their own—and each other's—strengths.…[It's] a good example to others who want to get the most out of their Net marketing bucks."

The most recent slate of Nike commercials encourages TV viewers to log onto the Nike Web site (*www.nike.com*) to choose a desired ending to its commercials. At the site, viewers can see several video clips with alternative endings. In addition, the site provides product information, humor, quizzes, stories, and online shopping opportunities. Unlike other e-commerce business, Nike has rejected the hard-sell approach. Instead, the emphasis is on Nike products as part of an individual's lifestyle. There is a definite sports theme, which makes sense, given Nike's product assortment, but the focus is on the Nike brand, not sports achievements. As a result, you won't find sports scores or sports news. Stories related to sports stars are written to be of interest to a broad cross section of customers. An article on Lance Armstrong, for instance, is potentially of interest to cycling fans, athletes, and cancer survivors.

But establishing its own Web site was just the start of Nike's online endeavors. A partnership with Web retailer Fogdog forged in late 1999 gave the e-company exclusive rights to sell Nike products online for several months. Fogdog, formerly sportsite.com, sells sports equipment and apparel, with footwear accounting for about one-third of its business. It currently carries approximately 160 Nike products, but will have the right to carry a much wider selection through the alliance.

Making its products available at a retail site separate from its own should significantly increase Nike's online shoe sales. Other Web retailers, such as Nordstrom, report that shoes sell well on the Internet, primarily because shoe sizes are more standardized than apparel sizes, so there is less of a concern about fit when ordering them.

KEEP THE ENTREPRENEURIAL SPIRIT ALIVE

Companies that evolve quickly—sometimes too quickly—from start-up to megacorporation face the challenge of keeping the entrepreneurial spirit alive within the organization. Although Nike's rise has been fast and furious—from nothing to $8 billion plus in less than three decades—the company has recognized the importance of passing along the story of its success. Several senior managers act as corporate storytellers, taking time to communicate tales of Nike's growth to the company's newest employees. Nelson Farris, Nike's director of corporate education and chief storyteller, explains in a recent issue of *Fast Company* that Nike's stories "are not about extraordinary business plans or financial manipulations. They're about people getting things done."

Stories about Bill Bowerman or past athletic stars are told to relate the company's heritage of innovation, commitment to helping athletes improve, and reliance on teamwork. In passing on these anecdotes, Nike helps its newest employees understand where the company has been and how it got to where it is today.

The storyteller program has it roots in the 1970s, when newly hired employees attended a one-hour corporate history lesson; today, that history lesson takes two days to tell and is referred to as an orientation program. A technical representative responsible for taking Nike's heritage on the road is called an "Ekin" ("Nike" spelled backward) and spends time bringing sales representatives at retailers such as Footlocker and Athlete's Foot into the fold.

And what is the goal of all this storytelling? It is to connect the people responsible for making, marketing, and selling Nike products to the company's heritage of helping athletes improve their performance. Understanding how and why that has come about is one way Nike keeps its corporate culture on course.

BE ON THE LOOKOUT FOR TRENDS

Aside from Nike's innovative designs, savvy alliances with sports celebrities, and cost-effective promotional program, the one factor that probably had more to do with the company's success than anything else is that Nike was started during the country's biggest fitness boom ever. Some might say that the company just got lucky. But it could also be argued that Knight recognized the increasing interest in his running shoes and took it as a sign of a shift in consumer interests.

The 1970s are known for a lot of things besides the start of Nike, including the start of jogging as a national pastime. By the end of the decade, approximately 48 percent of Americans had tried jogging.

Nike's auspicious start has much to do with Knight's love of running, which has kept him close to the customer for decades. And staying in touch with what his customers wanted helped to shift the company's focus when necessary.

WHAT NIKE WILL "JUST DO" NEXT

One of Nike's biggest challenges is keeping its trendy image youthful when consumers of all ages now wear its shoes. Another is to balance the edgy, in-your-face approach established with its "Just Do It" advertising mantra with a more approachable, friendly corporate image. Recent efforts indicate that the company is shifting toward a more grassroots appeal, rather than remaining dependent on celebrities, to make the Nike brand more personable.

Nike is also recognizing the increasing importance of the women's sports market and is ramping up its marketing program as a result. Female soccer stars Mia Hamm and Brandi Chastain will be joined by runner Marion Jones in promoting Nike wear. New products, such as the "Inner Actives" sports bra, are already gaining in popularity.

Monitoring the needs and desires of the worldwide athlete, rather than just the American market, will help to boost Nike's sales and establish it as a true global corporation.

PHIL'S MARKETING SECRETS

Be a sneaky genius, especially with new-product innovations.

Invest in marketing.

Align yourself with image leaders.

Donate a product.

Secure retail commitments.

Outsource production.

Face negative press head-on.

Get online.

Keep the entrepreneurial spirit alive.

Be on the lookout for trends.

REFERENCES

"Ads make Nike more approachable, but it's no longer true to its culture," by Rance Crain, *Advertising Age*, January 12, 1998.

"Anti-sweatshop effort at Nike to be expanded," by Joanna Ramey, *WWD*, May 12, 1998.

"Bowerman's legacy runs on," by Rosemary Feitelberg, *WWD*, December 30, 1999.

"Can Nike still do it?" *Business Week*, February 21, 2000.

"Casting Nike as the bad guy," by William Holstein, *U.S. News & World Report*, September 22, 1997.

"Defending a brand name," *Sales & Marketing Management*, September 1997.

"Demographics subject to rules of style," by Dick Silverman, *Footwear News*, April 5, 1999

"How Nike's brand is bouncing back," by Danny Rogers, *Marketing*, October 21, 1999.

"In the vanguard: trainers, sneakers and shoes," *The Economist*, June 7, 1997.

"Just doing it," by Adrian Murdoch, *Accountancy*, March 1999.

"Net gains," by Claude Solnik, *Footwear News*, December 6, 1999.

"Nike CEO vents at presentation of new anti-sweatshop efforts," by Joanna Ramey, *WWD*, May 13, 1998.

"Nike integration of TV, online a strong lesson," by Matt Carmichael, *Advertising Age*, February 14, 2000.

"Nike seals online retail deal with Redwood City, Calif. Company," by Andy Dworkin, *Knight-Ridder/Tribune Business News*, September 30, 1999.

"The Nike story? Just tell it," by Eric Ransdell, *Fast Company*, January/February 2000.

"Nike's Knight hits critics," by Georgia Lee, *WWD*, September 24, 1998.

"Nike wagers $90m on Woods being the next Jordan," by Francesca Newland, *Campaign*, September 3, 1999.

"Searching for answers amidst shrinking shares," by Terry Lefton, *Brandweek*, June 21, 1999.

"Surfing the hits," by Debra Carr, *Footwear News*, January 31, 2000.

Swoosh, by J.B. Strasser and Laurie Becklund, HarperBusiness, 1991.

"Swoosh shows signs of age as Nike tries to be hip again," by Gina Binole, *Business Journal-Portland*, April 3, 1998.

"Taking a commodity athletic shoe and turning it into a fashion statement took vision, edgy creativity, and a once-in-a-lifetime presenter named Mike," by Wayne Friedman, *Advertising Age*, December 13, 1999.

"Who's crying for Nike now that sales are off?" by Joe Cappo, *Crain's Chicago Business*, April 26, 1999.

CHAPTER THREE

MARKETING THE MATERIAL GIRL

Madonna

Some of the best marketers around today are performers and the people who manage them.

—Sergio Zyman
in *The End of Marketing as We Know It*

She is the greatest performing artist of her time.

—Norman Mailer,
as quoted in *Cosmopolitan*

INTRODUCTION

Famous, provocative, and sexy are frequently used to describe singer, dancer, actress, and producer Madonna. And yet, one of her biggest talents may indeed be her marketing know-how.

Few other performers have been able to capture public attention for as long as Madonna has. Going against the traditional marketing thinking that calls for consistency of image in order to develop a particular brand, Madonna regularly changes her looks—her packaging. Her hairstyle, hair color, wardrobe, and musical themes are constantly in flux, giving the public a different view of this versatile performer best known for her singing. Those changes are, in fact, what have made her remarkable.

Her ability to interest and even titillate the public is perhaps what has kept her career on an upswing for nearly on two decades. And by almost any standard, Madonna is an act that has been well marketed—she has sold more than 100 million albums worldwide and netted several more millions of dollars from her movie career. Her musical tours are frequently sold out, and her record label, Maverick, has been responsible for introducing and marketing several new performers.

MADONNA LOUISE VERONICA CICCONE—THE EARLY YEARS

Born in 1958, the third of six children to a Chrysler engineer and a homemaker, Madonna was traumatized at the age of five by the death of her mother. The emotional toll of her mother's premature death and her father's disciplinarian personality are two early experiences that shaped the type of woman—and performer—that she would become. Growing up, she reports, she was a good girl who felt very repressed, which many suggest may explain her focus on sexuality as a theme throughout her work.

The dance lessons she started at 13 would later launch her career, and her experience as a member of a rock band, the Breakfast Club, honed her musical abilities—but not as a vocalist: She was a guitarist and drummer in those days.

She left her father's house in Bay City, Michigan, in 1976 and enrolled at the University of Michigan on a dance scholarship, but left at age 20 to pursue a career in New York City. During the next six years in the Big Apple, she danced with Alvin Ailey and produced some dance tracks while living the life of a struggling artist.

Her big break came in 1984 in the form of a Sire Records deal. Her first hit, "Like a Virgin," led to her first movie, *Desperately Seeking Susan*, in 1985, which was followed by several straight-to-video types of film, including *Shanghai Surprise*, *Who's That Girl*, and *Body of Evidence*. Fortunately, she also had a role in the hit movie *Dick Tracy* in 1990 and in the critically acclaimed, "A League of Their Own," in 1992. Madonna considers her 1991 film *Truth or Dare*, a backstage look at show business, a success, but critics gave it mixed reviews. Her acting career earned its biggest boost when she won a Golden Globe award in 1996 for her role in *Evita*. However, her most recent movie production, *Next Best Thing*, wasn't released until 2000, primarily because of the birth of her daughter shortly after *Evita* was finished.

In between music hits like "Holiday," "Borderline," "Lucky Star," "Papa Don't Preach," and "Beautiful Stranger," Madonna found time to produce successful music videos and release her book, *Sex*, which is still of interest several years later. (Incidentally, the Omaha Public Library reports that there is always a waiting list for the "art book," years after its release.)

At 41 and a mother-to-be for the second time, Madonna continues to reflect our times as well as ever. Her latest album, "Ray of Light," expresses a newfound spirituality that many individuals are still seeking. And her latest role as mom links her with many of her baby boomer and Generation X fans who have, or are starting to have, families of their own.

Her ability to shape pop culture for almost two decades is a clear sign of her marketing prowess, for which she is frequently praised. Some of the moves she has made along the way include a number of success strategies you can use in your own business.

STRIVE FOR ACCEPTANCE BY IMAGE LEADERS

At the beginning of her singing career, Madonna recognized the importance of having her music accepted by image leaders: the black community. One of her earliest producers, Reggie Lucas, who wrote "Borderline" and produced her 1983 album debut, "Madonna," observes, "She was one of the first pop singers to deal with black music in a serious way. In fact, in the beginning it was most important to her to break a hit record in the black community, because she knew that would give her credibility throughout the entire industry."

Just as Phil Knight of Nike turned to professional athletes to provide credibility and demand for his sneakers, Madonna turned to image makers in the music industry to get her music off the ground. And the strategy paid off:

Almost from day one, her songs and videos have been popular among dancers, club goers, teenagers, college students, and virtually everyone in between. And as Madonna has grown up, her fans have grown up with her. Fortunately, she has also added to her base along the way, attracting audiences young and old. But without the acceptance and blessing of the black community, Madonna might still be a struggling artist.

BE WILLING TO BE CONTROVERSIAL

Although Madonna never set out specifically to be controversial, her steadfast dedication to speaking her mind has made her a notable figure, especially when she decides to address the issue of sexuality through her music and in print. Her pseudo-scandalous, as *Good Housekeeping* describes it, book, *Sex*, caused an uproar at its 1992 release. "The whole reason I got into show business wasn't because I thought I had a spectacular voice," she told an MTV interviewer. "It was because I thought I had something to say." While *Sex* was supposed to be ironic, not slutty, it generated plenty of word-of-mouth promotion because of its potentially pornographic portraits.

Through her music, Madonna has made a point of speaking her mind. "Papa Don't Preach," for example, addresses the issue of abortion head-on, and her "Like a Prayer" video angered religious groups for its use of burning crosses.

In her acting career, she has also been willing to take on nontraditional roles that have gotten tongues wagging. For example, her part of a gay witch in the movie *Four Rooms* raised eyebrows. Madonna, however, has no qualms about playing such parts, explaining, "It's a part in a movie, not my life."

While some performers might backtrack and ask for-
giveness for such actions in order to calm critics, Madonna
has never been one to apologize. She stands by her music
and her message, which is perhaps the reason her fans like
her so much.

SEX SELLS

We've all heard that sex sells and nowhere is this more evident than in Madonna's career. She could be called the
poster girl for blatant sexuality. Although her early image
(remember "Material Girl") positioned her more as an outspoken character than as a pinup girl, over time she mor-
phed into a highly sexual creature. Starting with "Like a
Virgin," when she writhed on stage in a big bed as part of
her video, and later to her "Blonde Ambition" tour, where
she dressed as a vamp in a pink bustier, and more recently
with "Erotica," her 1992 highly suggestive album, sex and
Madonna became intertwined. "I don't regret having dealt
with sexuality so often and so openly in my work....Unfor-
tunately, *s-e-x* became my moniker, even though almost all
of my songs are romantic," she says.

Although she's backed off of her emphasis on sex to sell
her music, Madonna will always be best known for her willingness to make her sexuality an integral part of her public persona. Even offscreen and outside of her music,
Madonna has always been one to be risqué—dating former
playboy Warren Beatty and controversial Dennis Rodman
got people talking about her, too. It seemed that she was
attracted only to men with a bad reputation. But that may
be behind her now.

In a recent *Good Housekeeping* article, she admits, "I
did my sexual rebellion thing. I took it as far as I could go.
I shaved my eyebrows. I've been naked in every state and

country. . . . I've dated the NBA. I mean, there's nothing more!"

NEVER GROW COMPLACENT

Part of Madonna's appeal, perhaps, is her willingness to take risks, to try new styles and musical approaches. Former producer Lucas points out, "When you listen to [Madonna's] early hits, she was willing to take chances with her voice and her material that people with trained, or more conventionally 'good,' voices would do."

She also has not been one to be content with her current standing in the music or entertainment industry. Whereas many entertainers focus so long and so hard on becoming stars that they often fade out shortly after achieving their goal, Madonna's vision has always been to have an ongoing, lasting role. Instead of resting on her laurels, Madonna is always interested in showcasing new looks, styles, images, and public personas to keep her audience on its feet. She has used shock value repeatedly to keep her name on people's tongues and her music on the charts.

BE WILLING TO UPDATE THE PACKAGING REGULARLY

To keep interest alive and fans—as well as the critics—talking, Madonna has been the quintessential chameleon. She reinvents herself constantly, keeping audiences guessing about who she'll be next. Changing and updating her image on a regular basis, in sync with her newest musical style, has kept audiences buying her records for years. Even after most musical acts have fallen by the wayside, Madonna continues to entertain and interest a broad audience after close to

20 years. Even Madonna herself has remarked that she is "her own experiment, her own work of art; a woman who has grown, improved, transformed," says *Cosmopolitan*.

Keeping content fresh and new is a theme heard repeatedly in reference to one of the newest marketing tools: the Web site. Current wisdom is that, to keep visitors coming back, Webmasters have to offer updated information on a regular basis. Well, Madonna was certainly one of the first modern-day marketers to live by that rule. And today, Web visitors use the technology to keep up to date on Madonna happenings and music.

Subjects she has addressed through her music have been varied, as has the look she has adopted to support her image. She started as the material girl, compliments of one of her first hits, then grew into the strong-willed woman she played in *Desperately Seeking Susan* and the dark-haired siren who sang about religion in "Like a Prayer," then became the blonde who preferred teddies and bustiers during her "Blonde Ambition" tour and the blonde who liked *sadomasochism* (S&M) in "Erotica," and wound up as the accomplished, more polished woman who played Evita in the movie of the same name and, more recently, the spiritual songstress with dark hair again who sings "Ray of Light."

Of late, her image of wholesome mom has come through media appearances in which she speaks of her daughter. Her movie, *The Next Best Thing*, deals with parenting issues. And her June Cleaverish cover picture on *Good Housekeeping* signals her new transformation.

HIRE THE BEST

In the music industry, it is the producer who has the most control over the final product. And yet, few singers or musicians appear to give credit where credit is due. According to early producer Reggie Lucas, Madonna always gave her producers public credit. And she has worked with many of the best, including Jellybean Benitez and Patrick Leonard.

In several cases, it was the producers who helped her create new variations of existing songs, such as dance remixes. And those producers are certainly partially responsible for the level of success Madonna has achieved.

KEEP EXPANDING YOUR TARGET MARKET

Clearly, the dance remixes aided her efforts to expand her audience. Whereas her initial fan club consisted primarily of teenyboppers, over time she has been able to draw in a broad cross section of consumers—from the dance club crowd, to MTV devotees, to middle-aged moviegoers—through her various morphs from material girl to spiritualist and from struggling actress to awardwinner.

As most marketers know, there are three basic ways to increase revenues: by selling more products to existing customers, by selling higher value products to existing customers, and by selling products to new customers. Madonna, of course, has implemented programs to boost revenues in all three areas. She regularly produces new albums to meet demand from existing fans, creates new streams of revenue —such as performances and movies— that are more expensive than albums, and reinvents herself periodically to gain new audiences. Most companies focus only on one of these areas, but Madonna goes squarely at all three, which is probably why she's worth millions. Called "the most significant female performer pop culture has produced in the past half century," Madonna has achieved icon status by combining sexuality, a now-strong singing voice, and a constantly shifting public persona.

PAY MORE ATTENTION TO YOUR CUSTOMERS THAN TO THE CRITICS

Despite the fact that she has sold more than 100 million records and won music video honors, Grammy awards, and a Golden Globe, Madonna has not yet won over all her critics. Some blast her acting abilities, while others trash her music, her message, or her look. Fortunately, she is oblivious to them all.

Had she paid attention to the critics, she would have put aside her ambitions long ago. In 1984, with the release of "Like a Virgin," her second album, following "Madonna" in 1983, she was "dismissed by critics as a tarty flash in the pan," reports *People Weekly*. Her vocal abilities, as well as her acting talent, have been panned, but instead of daunting Madonna, such comments have served only to fuel her desire to improve.

She has been unwilling to change her style or her message to appease concerned consumer groups and critics, generating additional controversy that has further boosted her notoriety. In fact, her R-rated performances, which have been banned in some cities, may draw more crowds because of efforts to keep people from seeing them. Likewise, *Sex* caused an uproar when it was published, with some bookstores banning it from their shelves. All that this contoversy served to do was heighten curiosity and demand.

More recently, Madonna earned the wrath of some Hindus following her appearance at the 1998 MTV awards as the Hindu god Shiva, as part of her performance of "Ray of Light." Apparently, her makeup, which resembled Hindu facial markings that suggest purity and devotion, contrasted offensively with the translucent top she wore and sexy dancing she performed. Once again, the publicity surrounding the gaffe—which may have been entirely planned—has raised awareness of her new album and increased interest in the art of painting hands and faces with ink.

But Madonna does admit that the comments of critics and media personalities sometimes hurt. In an interview in *Cosmopolitan*, she was asked whether she pays attention to the media: "If you mean do I sit at home wishing I'd done it all differently so they'd love me, no. But I do pay attention to the sexism and the cruelty and negativity of it." Throughout all her experiences, Madonna seems amazingly able to learn from them—good and bad—and move forward, ready to take on a new challenge. "I can only hope that if I'm patient and diligent enough, if I continue to grow as an artist and a human being, people will come to realize that I'm not some callous, power-hungry, sex-crazed control freak who sings occasionally." Her resiliency is also part of her appeal to many fans, despite what critics or the media say.

INVEST IN SUPPORTING PRODUCTS

Madonna's co-ownership of Maverick Records with Time Warner, a label known for hot, young musicians such as pop singer Alanis Morissette, funk rocker Me'Shell Ndegeocello, and heavy rock band Candlebox, is one strategy for extending her influence in the music industry. Although Madonna herself may not perform forever, especially with two children in tow, her involvement in Maverick will enable her to profit from up-and-coming stars as much as support them.

Me'Shell has sold several hundred thousand copies of her first two Maverick releases, Candlebox has sold 3.4 million copies of its 1993 release of its album by the same name, and Morissette has sold more than 20 million copies of her debut album, "Jagged Little Pill." Its 1996 revenues were approximately $100 million, up from $56 million in 1995, with profits nearly doubling.

Maverick can also extend Madonna's reign as one of the most influential performers of her time. While known most for her music, she has also gained a following of movie fans. Fashion magazine *W* ranks Madonna third in its list of America's most-coveted party guests.

MADONNA AT FORTY-SOMETHING

Despite spending many years in the entertainment industry, Madonna now seems satisfied to play the role of mom for a while. No, this is not a publicity stunt or another marketing transformation; it's simply a new phase in Madonna's life. She explains that her new role has put limitations on what she's willing to do, however: "There are a lot of things I can't—not won't, can't—do anymore because I have a kid."

Little Lourdes Maria Ciccone Leon will be raised Catholic without the influence of television or the Internet, says her mother, which is ironic, given the impact those two media have had on Madonna's career: She is one of the most-downloaded celebrities online and has made millions as a result of her music videos and performances.

But with an estimated fortune of $200 million, she can surely afford to redirect her attention away from work for a bit. But don't expect her to retire—just to return later with new packaging!

MADONNA'S MARKETING MANTRA
Strive for acceptance by image leaders.
Be willing to be controversial.
Sex sells.
Never grow complacent.
Be willing to update the packaging regularly.
Hire the best.
Keep expanding your target market.
Pay more attention to your customers than to the critics.
Invest in supporting products.

REFERENCES

"Do the 'light' thing," *Entertainment Weekly*, March 20, 1998.

The End of Marketing as We Know It, by Sergio Zyman, HarperBusiness, 1999.

"Lady Madonna," *People Weekly*, March 13, 2000.

"Madonna," by Ken Tucker, *Entertainment Weekly*, November 1, 1999.

"Madonna: A self-styled experiment in sexuality," by Dennis Ferrara, *Cosmopolitan*, February 1996.

"Madonna: The mother of reinvention set a new standard of female fame," by Steve Dougherty, *People Weekly*, March 15, 1999.

"Madonna grows up," by Liz Smith, *Good Housekeeping*, April 2000.

"Madonna on life before and after motherhood," by Peter Wilkinson, *Redbook*, January 1997.

"Madonna's hedge," by Robert La Franco, *Forbes*, September 23, 1996.

"New day, new deity to offend," *Time*, September 28, 1998.

"The season of the diva," by Judith Timson, *Maclean's*, March 8, 1999.

"They want your 'sex,'" by Casey Davidson, *Entertainment Weekly*, August 16, 1996.

CHAPTER FOUR

MARKETING
THE ART OF LIVING

Martha Stewart

Media companies regard Martha Stewart Living Omnimedia *as the guiding light for how to turn brands into multiple platforms for consumers with specific interests.*
—Advertising Age

Martha Stewart is perhaps the country's preeminent female brand name.
—The New York Times

INTRODUCTION

Called everything from the "Diva of Domesticity" to "America's Lifestyle Queen," Martha Stewart has earned both the respect and animosity of the American public for her advice on the household arts. But no matter whether you're a Martha fan or foe, you can't help but admire her ability to grow her company, Martha Stewart Living Omnimedia, LLC (MSLO), at breakneck speed.

Martha can be credited, first and foremost, with turning the convenience trend of the 1970s and 1980s—when it comes to cooking, cleaning, decorating, and sewing—on its heels. She made it chic again to care about the appearance of a gift, to select just the right shade of pale blue paint for the walls, or to shop for the freshest vegetables for the evening's meal. As *People Weekly* comments, "Hers is a comforting, almost nostalgic aesthetic, one that seeks to re-create a world in which there were no cake mixes, no microwaves, no IKEA." Single-handedly, Martha Stewart rejuvenated the field of "homekeeping," as she likes to call it.

EARLY INFLUENCES

Born Martha Helen Kostyra in 1941 in Jersey City, New Jersey, the woman who would later redefine the American lifestyle attained many of her skills from her family. It was her paternal grandfather who may have instilled a love of cooking in her, reports Jerry Oppenheimer in *Martha Stewart—Just Desserts*, while her father passed along his fascination with gardening, sewing, and design. Later, husband Andy Stewart's mother, Ethel, introduced Martha to antiques and auctions.

She was also tremendously ambitious, stating early on her goal to be a nationally recognized personality. Friends marveled at her ability to succeed in schoolwork, modeling, and extracurricular activities all at the same time. This ability to juggle multiple projects continues to serve Martha well as she introduces new products and adds new ventures to her growing empire. Her reign as queen of the domestic arts began with a career in catering. Actually, Martha had decided in grade school that she wanted to be a caterer, claims a friend. After learning what a caterer was, Martha immediately determined what she would charge, what she would serve, and how she would operate her business. In fact, she began approaching neighbors for business. Once she decided what she wanted, she moved quickly to attain it, in what would become known as typical Martha style.

After completing college at Barnard and marrying Andy Stewart, Martha settled into a traditional life for a while, before beginning a career as a stockbroker. Although she was successful as a stockbroker, Martha eventually quit the field to start a catering business, called The Uncatered Affair, in the mid-1970s. From there, she took over a retail food business, naming it The Market Basket. The company prepared meals for couples to pick up on their way home from work. These two ventures introduced many New York-area families to the name Martha Stewart and began associating her with good food and trendy entertaining. Through word of mouth and some targeted local publicity moves, Martha quickly gained a reputation as a talented caterer.

At the same time that Martha embarked on her new career, her husband Andy made a career switch into publishing, giving her the impetus and connections that would make it feasible to consider writing her own cookbook. But it was Andy's first major publishing success that would teach Martha some valuable marketing lessons.

MAXIMIZE MERCHANDISING

Martha's biggest marketing breakthrough came rather early in her career as a caterer, according to Oppenheimer. It was the 1970s and then-husband Andy had taken on the challenge of marketing an unusual book about fairies and gnomes. It would be one of his biggest hits, in part because of the tremendous revenue generated from ancillary products featuring the book's characters. The book, *Gnomes*, did very well, selling millions in its first year of publication. But the canvas book bags, ceramic figures, posters, notepads, and towels brought in significant additional revenue. And this was not lost on Martha. On the contrary, she immediately recognized the potential for extending a brand, which is what *Gnomes* had become, and set about applying the same principle to the various facets of her catering business.

Developing merchandising opportunities in the form of related products that could be packaged and sold under her brand name became part of the magical Martha Stewart formula that has worked so well. Today, there are more than 2800 Martha-branded products.

"The [business] concept is one of enabling, freeing up the desire to cook, decorate, garden in your home," says MSLO President Sharon Patrick. "[Customers] need the tools, products and materials to do it." And Martha is just the woman to sell it to them.

She went from a caterer that sold and served gourmet food to much more. And she began developing product ideas that could generate add-on sales through her existing distribution channels, namely, a retail store and catering operation. Expanding the number of channels open to her would come later.

In 1999, books, magazines, and publishing activities generated approximately 71 percent of the company's revenues, with TV and radio contributing 13 percent and merchandising royalties adding another 10 percent—up from 0 just a few years before.

PURSUE POSITIVE PUBLICITY

In 1979, as a result of the buzz about the New York caterer, *People Magazine* did a story on Martha, positioning her as a lifestyle expert. This event, combined with her growing familiarity with the publishing world, was the start of Martha's life as how-to information provider. Following the article's publication, Martha was asked to submit occasional articles about food, gardening, entertaining, and decorating to such publications as *Good Housekeeping* and *Country Living*—well-respected lifestyle magazines. And based on the success of those articles, she was hired as freelance food editor for *House Beautiful* for a short period, improving her publishing credentials. The opportunity to write such articles provided Martha with credibility and prestige that no amount of advertising or promotional material could accomplish. The implied endorsement of such high-powered publications was priceless, especially to a caterer with an eye on establishing herself as a brand.

Part of the reason Martha Stewart has become ubiquitous in the past few years is her strategy of doggedly pursuing publicity. Media coverage has been very good for business and has cost a fraction of what the same amount of advertising would have sold for. Even when poking fun at herself—remember the American Express Card ad showing her seated in her pool, cutting up credit cards to line the bottom?—Martha exudes an elegance and class that many Americans aspire to have.

Comparisons are frequently made between Julia Child, the superchef of the 1960s, and Martha, the larger-than-life home expert of the 1990s—and beyond. While there are certainly similarities (both are known for their cooking skills, and both have had cooking shows and best-selling books), there is one major difference: Julia Child is a one-hit wonder compared with the multifaceted Martha.

Content to be put on a pedestal as the world's best-known chef, Julia never leveraged the power of her name the way that Martha has. Where Julia was, and is, clearly a well-known personality—even a celebrity—Martha's power extends beyond that. Her influence is felt in entertaining, decorating, home organizing, gardening, sewing, home maintenance, and wedding planning, as well as in cooking. To some, she is a cultural icon, to many, a quality brand name.

BUILD YOUR BRAND

Today, the core concept of taking a brand or a product and extending it into new markets is at the heart of the success of the Martha Stewart brand. In fact, some would call it a new business model. Never before has a brand achieved such reach in so many forms. Martha herself has become an icon of the entertaining and decorating world because she grasped early on the importance of establishing and mining a brand identity. In her case, Martha Stewart *is* the brand.Where she started with guest appearances on local television programs, Martha moved up to national programming and is now a regular on "CBS This Morning." She then took that experience and pursued her own television show, "Martha Stewart Living," which has recently been joined by a second show, "From Martha's Kitchen," which, after just a few months is already the top-rated weekday show on the Food Network among her target market: women 25–54.

But why limit herself solely to television? Indeed, Martha has penetrated virtually every media outlet that exists today. In addition to her television program, she has a radio show, a syndicated newspaper column, two magazines, a Web site, a direct-marketing catalog, and a book-publishing venture consisting of 27 titles—and counting. In total, her media properties reach more than 88 million people a month, and that's not even counting her syndicated newspaper column!

Martha also has her own line of products, from home décor and bedding products sold through Kmart, to a line of paints—Martha Stewart Everyday Colors—available at Sears, to smaller household accessories touted in her magazine, *Martha Stewart Living*, and in her mail-order catalog, *Martha By Mail*.

Martha Stewart Living has a circulation of nearly 2.3 million subscribers, her books have sold 8.5 million copies, and 1998 revenues from household, paint, and mail-order products hit $763 million in revenue, according to a November 1999 *Brill's Content* article.

In January 2000, Martha launched marthasflowers.com as a means of extending her brand identity into the lucrative $15 billion floral industry. Used frequently in entertaining and decorating, floral arrangements are a natural tie-in to the Martha Stewart lifestyle her fans strive for. And on the marketing side, establishing e-commerce outlets directly related to her identity as entertainment guru makes a lot of sense.

Taking her company public in 1999 raised $149 million in financing and made Martha a billionaire on paper. Part of the reason for that success may be that MSLO is one of the very few companies to show a profit from the start. Sales exceeded $225 million for 1999 and are expected to reach $400 million by 2003.

PARTNER WITH ESTABLISHED DISTRIBUTION CHANNELS

Just as Martha Stewart has created several vehicles to dispense her homekeeping message, she has also strategically aligned herself with several well-established retailers with the power to push her products. Kmart was her first alliance, begun in 1987, when Martha Stewart was just barely a lifestyle personality. And although some marketing gurus disagree on whether such a partnership makes sense for the upscale Martha brand, clearly the arrangement has benefited both parties. In 1999, Kmart sold more than $1 billion worth of Martha Stewart products, including Martha Stewart Everyday linens and accessories and the Martha Stewart Everyday Baby line.

Currently in the works is the establishment of Martha Stewart Everyday boutiques within Kmart's 2145 stores, where the retailer will set aside approximately 4500 square feet per store solely for Martha to market and sell her branded wares to Kmart customers. The Kmart relationship has meant not only increasing revenue for MSLO, but increasing familiarity and reach among the lower and middle-income consumers who shop at Kmart. Broader distribution helps Martha appeal to the masses, further building the legions of "marthamaniacs" who adore her products and decorating style.

Kmart, however, is by no means the only MSLO partner. The company has alliances with Zellers, a Canadian mass market discounter similar to Kmart; Sears and Canadian

Tire, which provide an entrée into the national department store arena; and Calico Corners and Jo-Ann Fabric and Crafts, which are MSLO's link to the specialty retail channel. On the manufacturing front, Sherwin-Williams actually produces a Martha Stewart line of paints, as well as Fine Paints of Europe, and P/Kaufman produces the new line of decorative home fabrics.

BE A TRENDSETTER

Martha always had a knack for being ahead of the curve in terms of discovering and establishing new trends, according to her friends in *Martha Stewart—Just Desserts*. Just as the market began to shift away from one fad, Martha was already onto something else. And her timing was just as impeccable with the publication of her first book, *Entertaining*, in 1982. Incidentally, *Entertaining* is now in its 30th printing, proving the popularity of both the subject matter and the author.

According to food writer and critic Richard Sax in *Just Desserts*, "Martha did *Entertaining* at the exact epicenter, the exact moment, when things were bursting out all over the place in the food world….The food revolution was happening in terms of people being exposed to new and different kinds of cooking….Martha was in the right place at the right time with the right idea."

EMBRACE TECHNOLOGY

Staying ahead of trends requires that Martha stay at the leading edge of information technology, which she claims makes it possible for her to accomplish as much as she does in a day. Investing in the latest and greatest technology for her homes, studio, and office enables information to be shared across her rapidly growing organization, keeping production schedules on course. "Technology makes it possible, so it's going to get done," she says.

Just some of the technology Martha has incorporated into her life are 10 phone lines in her Westport, Connecticut, home, a cell phone that accompanies her wherever she goes, a desktop Macintosh computer, a Powerbook for traveling, two laser printers, and a fax machine. While being driven to the office, Martha makes use of a Sony MiniDisc Recorder to dictate instructions to her staff and to note ideas for stories.

In the conference room of the Martha Stewart Living Omnimedia offices, Martha has installed a state-of-the-art video teleconferencing system that enables her to attend out-of-town board meetings when she can't get away.But her commitment to technology goes beyond investing in it to be more productive: Martha was also one of the first corporate marketers to see the tremendous potential of e-commerce.

Her company's Web site, marthastewart.com, is frequently used as a case study of how to effectively grow an online business. The site itself is organized into seven core content areas—cooking and entertaining, gardening, home, crafts, housekeeping, holidays, and weddings—that "define MSLO's lifestyle focus," explains the company's prospectus. Within each area, visitors will find how-to information, dispensed Martha style.

Part of the reason that the site has grown so large so fast is that it has so many promotional outlets to drive traffic to it. Television viewers see the Web address during program segments, radio listeners hear the site's URL during the "askMartha" show, and readers of *Martha Stewart Living* see ads for the Web site sprinkled throughout the magazine. Few—if any—media conglomerates can provide the reach that MSLO does for its Web site.

From the beginning, Martha recognized that to attract and keep visitors coming back to the site, she had to give them information that was useful and could be acted upon. So, in addition to viewing a well-designed site that reflects the look and feel of the magazine, visitors can download recipes, check the program guide to learn what topics will be covered in upcoming TV shows, retrieve instructions on completing projects featured on TV, and access the Martha By Mail Web store, enabling them to purchase tools and accessories online.

Most importantly, however, marthastewart.com has asked for the email addresses of its visitors from the start, giving the company the opportunity to recontact those visitors with special offers and reminders. By providing their email addresses, visitors gain access to online discussion groups, earn the chance to enter sweepstakes, and can receive a weekly bulletin from Martha. By August 1999, the site had 1,000,000 registered users and, along with sales from the Martha By Mail catalog, accounted for roughly 18 percent of the company's revenues.

DELEGATE TO THE EXPERTS

Although Martha Stewart the person is synonymous with the MSLO organization, the company is aggressively trying to reduce its reliance on her, both as a personality and as provider of information. Whereas Martha formerly developed all of the content ideas for the company, there are now in-house creative experts who have been hired to assume that responsibility. All told, MSLO has a staff of more than 160 of these experts and an estimated 240 more workers.

The company's reliance on Martha's image is also being significantly reduced. The most obvious sign is that she no longer appears on the cover of the magazine. She is also encouraging her team leaders to assume a more visible role in the various media outlets.

As MSLO's Sharon Patrick explains in a recent issue of *Advertising Age*, "Martha was the visionary and the driver of understanding the power of how-to content. Martha stands for what this brand is, and is instrumental in presenting it. It's moving from trusted personality to trusted products and services. The branded product becomes the next step."

REPACKAGE AND REPURPOSE INFORMATION

Undoubtedly, one of Martha Stewart's strengths is her ability to do several things at once. This is true in her personal life, where she is known as a dynamo who can't stand still, and at her company, where each piece of how-to information is used several times over, in various forms.

A magazine article is never just a magazine article. Nor is a TV segment just a one-time program. For example, an article on creating a festive holiday wreath can also be used as a chapter in an upcoming holiday decorating book she may publish and as a segment on her television show and radio program. In addition, it can be mentioned in her syndicated newspaper column, listed as a program item on the Web site, and packaged as a do-it-yourself kit sold through Martha By Mail.

Reusing and repackaging information in numerous forms is much more profitable than using it once and setting it aside, as so many media companies do. In fact, approximately 60 percent of the material presented in Martha's books is culled from *Martha Stewart Living*. So in many respects, revenue from the books is gravy—the incremental cost to reformat the material into a book is minimal, hence, keeping costs down.

WHAT'S NEXT FOR MARTHA STEWART

This savvy marketer plans to continue building her brand through new merchandise in the coming year, introducing a new housewares line for Kmart and exploring the possibilities for a gardening and outdoor-product line. But her true strength lies in her ability to attract more and more fans; some critics refer to them as "cultlike" in their enthusiasm for her and her products. Truly, though, this is an asset, not a liability. As a *New York Times* reporter asserts, "Ms. Stewart manages to give her readers the sense that she is one of them. In this way, she embodies the very paradox that magazine publishers are constantly seeking: giving readers something impossible to aspire to, yet something real they can relate to."

MARTHA'S MARKETING PRINCIPLES

Maximize merchandise.
Pursue positive publicity.
Build your brand at every opportunity.
Partner with established distribution channels.
Be a trendsetter.
Embrace technology for communications and sales.
Delegate to the experts.
Repackage and repurpose information.

REFERENCES

"Grand Design," by Calmetta Coleman, *Wall Street Journal*, May 1, 2000.

"The Influence List," *Brill's Content*, November 1999, p. 95.

"How to Market by Email," by Deborah Spence, *FOLIO: The Magazine for Magazine Management*, January 1999.

"A Living Brand," by Ann Smith, *Progressive Grocer*, November 1998.

"Martha Inc.," *Business Week*, January 17, 2000, p. 63.

Martha Stewart—Just Desserts, by Jerry Oppenheimer, William Morrow, 1997.

"Master of Her Own Destiny," by Robin Pogrebin, *New York Times*, February 8, 1998.

"The War of the Roses," *Time*, February 21, 2000.

CHAPTER FIVE

THE AYA-COLA OF COCA-COLA

Sergio Zyman

Marketers have forgotten and need to remember real soon... that marketing is about selling stuff. Marketing is not about creating an image. Having an image just means that I know who you are, but it doesn't motivate me to do anything.

—Sergio Zyman
in *The End of Marketing as We Know It*

INTRODUCTION

Forget all you've heard about the utter failure of New Coke, says marketing guru Sergio Zyman: It was actually a stunning success. While those outside Coca-Cola, and some inside, viewed the brief life span of New Coke as a downright fiasco, Zyman argues that the product's introduction did exactly what it was supposed to: reclaim the relationship between Coke and consumers. In other words, it sold Coke. Lots of it. And that's exactly what it was supposed to do. Granted, he admits, the introduction didn't go as planned, but in the end, the marketing worked.

The success or failure of New Coke, depending on how you look at it, speaks volumes about Sergio Zyman as Coke's marketing chief and about how he views the function of marketing.

Sometimes arrogant, often provocative, and certainly opinionated, Zyman has been credited with some of the company's largest successes, as well as having achieved substantial sales and earnings gains during his 13-year tenure.

THE AYA-COLA'S REIGN

Zyman led Coca-Cola's marketing department for more than a decade, from 1979 to 1987 and then again from 1993 to 1998, boosting its global product sales from 9 to 15 billion cases in the space of just five years. When Zyman joined Coke in 1993 for a second stint as head of marketing, the brand's share of the U.S. soft-drink market was 40.7 percent; five years later the figure had risen to 43.9 percent. At the same time, the company's stock price rose from $20 per share to more than $76, even after a split in 1996. Although Zyman is best known for New Coke, he also was responsible for the tremendously successful "Coke is It" slogan and is credited with tripling Sprite's sales in just four years by repositioning the soft drink. In addition, he is responsible for the introduction of Diet Coke, which is one of the company's leading products today.

In the beginning, however, there was just one product, Coca-Cola, a five-cent bottle of carbonated sweetness that was originally invented as a tonic for stomach upset. Through the years, much has changed. The company has grown, increased its product offerings, and expanded into geographic markets worldwide. Coca-Cola Co. is now a $19.8 billion company, with close to 29,000 employees. At the end of Zyman's reign, the company was selling more than 1 billion servings of its products daily in more than 196 countries. Volume was growing at an average of 7 percent per year. But today, the numbers are not nearly as strong: Coke's global volume grew just 1 percent in 1999, while its operating profits fell 20 percent. Clearly, the company has had better days, namely, when Zyman was in charge of its marketing.

HAVE A GAME PLAN

"Strategy is everything," says Zyman —more important than advertising, more important than packaging, perhaps even more important than the product itself. "Decide where you want to go, and then build your objectives, strategies, and plans to get you there." Zyman's position is

"DESTINATION"

that marketing is a science, a discipline built on systematic approaches and measurable results. "It is not an art," he retorts. So it follows that this science would consist of specific action items, all designed to convince people to buy what you have to sell. And those action items, in turn, would be based on thorough research about the customer, the market, the environment, and the competition. But since profitability is the goal, you can't pursue every potential market. That would be much too expensive, and many markets simply aren't worth the effort. So your strategy must lay out a plan to increase sales as efficiently and cost effectively as possible. What is your number-one objective? That is, what is your destination? Whatever it is, it should ultimately provide improved profitability. Otherwise, why does your company exist?

From that number-one objective—your destination—follows your strategy for reaching it. The strategy will keep you on the straight and narrow when you might be tempted to implement a new approach that could lead you far afield from your destination. And from that strategy follows tactics—action items that propel you toward your destination through the strategy you have laid out.

To illustrate the concepts of strategy and tactics, Zyman uses the example of Microsoft's introduction of Internet Explorer. He says that following Netscape's release of its Navigator search engine, Microsoft sought to neutralize its competitor's product by giving away its own product. Microsoft's strategy was to "knock Navigator out of the market by making it obsolete."

SUCCESS EQUALS INCREASED SALES

In his book, *The End of Marketing as We Know It*, Zyman explains how marketing has gone astray. Instead of providing strong reasons for people to buy products and services, companies are stuck on building awareness; but awareness doesn't give someone a reason to buy. "The sole purpose of marketing is to sell more to more people, more often, and at higher prices," he states. And he is true to his principles: Throughout Zyman's career at Coke, the measure he used to assess the success or failure of his marketing initiatives was whether product sales had increased. Nothing else was as important. Remember the heartwarming ad featuring football star Mean Joe Greene being given a Coke by a small boy? Or the catchy "I'd like to teach the world to sing" ad showing crowds of people walking over a hill singing? Chances are you do, because these two ads quickly became favorites. Consumers loved them. Zyman, on the other hand, hated them and canceled them shortly after they aired. Why? You guessed it: They didn't improve sales.

Before the information age and the proliferation of technology, creating awareness of a product *was* the goal of marketing. At that time, increasing awareness and familiarity with a product was enough. But today, there's just too much clutter. We're assaulted daily with too much information; it's virtually impossible for a product to stand out and be memorable. Consequently, marketing's objectives have changed—from building awareness to generating sales. In order to capture consumers' attention, there has to be a harder push for sales; to cut through information clutter, you need to be more direct. Give consumers an explicit reason to buy your product.

Some marketers argue that a company or product must first establish an image—that image building in and of itself, is a goal. This was certainly the thinking during the 1980s, but according to Zyman, those days are over. "Marketing is not about creating an image," he explains. "Having an image just means I know who you are, but it doesn't motivate me to do anything."

ADVERTISE BENEFITS

Zyman's mantra that marketing must result in sales also applies to promotional tools, such as advertising. Ads in which product benefits are not clearly communicated can serve to confuse consumers and certainly don't affect sales in any significant way. Examples of Coke ads that didn't hit the mark are the 1998 Super Bowl promos for Coke Classic. Instead of reminding consumers of reasons to drink Coke Classic, the goofy ads focused on Coke's link with the color red, including nicknames for redheads. Needless to say, the ads were neither memorable nor goal-oriented, and their performance, which was evaluated through surveys, was abysmal. Since then, other ads have been entertaining, but only recently has the company returned to highlighting reasons to buy Coke in its advertising.

RESEARCH, RESEARCH, RESEARCH

The only way to make your marketing more effective is to analyze both the past and the future, states Zyman. Research makes it possible to constantly refine and improve the quality of your marketing. Evaluating the results of past marketing strategies enables you to learn what went right and what went wrong, so that you move forward, are able to apply the tactics that worked, and eliminate those that didn't. Zyman's success formula is "Assume, experiment, review and revise." And since marketing is an ongoing process, rather than a one-time event, any aspect of a marketing strategy can be researched with this formula. The results will then improve the odds of success.

Even outright failures can be learning experiences, as was the case with the introduction of OK Soda, one of the

company's duds. The pepper-flavored soda was ignored by its target market —teens—but taught the marketing team how to better interact with younger audiences. Those insights have since been used to promote Barq's Root Beer, for instance, and to develop Web-related activities for Cherry Coke.

By the same token, looking to the future and asking "What if?" is equally important. Although marketers typically look to the past in order to make plans for the future, Zyman proposes looking forward and asking hypothetical questions as a better approach. He calls this forward-looking, hypothesis-based research "presearch."

In his book, Zyman makes an analogy between political pollsters and marketers: "A good campaign manager goes a step further by doing presearch. In other words, he or she asks voters: What if we told you this tomorrow? Would you vote for the candidate? And they keep asking until they find the positioning that is going to move votes....Marketers need to do the same thing."

Coke, fortunately, has been a leader in getting at why consumers buy certain products, including its own. But the company has also studied other products, often for the benefit of their distribution partners. In fact, Coke's research acumen is used as a negotiating point in structuring partnerships with other companies. Wendy's, for example, switched from Pepsi to Coke in a 10-year deal, in part because of Coke's research capabilities. "What sealed the deal was the added value of an exclusive partnership with Coke," says Wendy's spokesman Denny Lynch in a *Sales and Marketing Management* article. "While Coke picks up more than 700 franchises that were previously served by Pepsi, Wendy's gets a cross-functional team of 50 Coke employees in various regions of the country who are now dedicated to 'understanding the nuances of Wendy's business.'"

Coke invests heavily in research to better understand the buying motives of its target audiences and makes that research available to its partners. According to *Sales and Marketing Management*, the company has analyzed the demographics of every zip code in the United States, using that information as the basis for a software program called Solver. Franchise owners who are Coke distributors can use the software to determine which Coke brands are preferred by consumers in their area. But Coke goes beyond just studying the public's beverage-drinking habits, seeking to help its partners in almost any area of their business. Coke has been known to research effective hiring practices for those of its partners facing difficulties during periods of low unemployment.

NEUTRALIZE THE COMPETITION

Sometimes a product should be introduced with the goal of failure, suggests Zyman. Such situations arise when the competition introduces a product that interferes with your products' ability to be profitable. By developing a rival to a competitor's product, you gain the opportunity to reposition the competitor's product by comparing it with your own. And in doing so, you can confuse the market. Such was the case with Tab Clear, a Coke product launched specifically to hurt Pepsi's Crystal Pepsi. Tab Clear was never expected to do well. In fact, the goal was to have it die out quickly, but only after confusing the market and killing off the clear cola category. What's the benefit of this, you ask? The answer is that by shutting down a new carbonated beverage category—clear colas—Coke preserved the market share of its existing brands. "We didn't think that the category was ever going to be big enough to make economic sense, but it was an annoyance and a diversion of consumers' interest."

Coke's strategy was to reposition Crystal Pepsi as a diet cola, where it had a major competitive *dis*advantage: It contained sugar. So, compared with all the other diet drinks, Crystal Pepsi was a dud. Consumers became confused about what Crystal Pepsi's unique selling proposition (USP) was: Was it a diet drink? Was the taste preferable? Was clear better than brown-colored colas? As a result, the category got muddied and Crystal Pepsi died out. Likewise, Tab Clear was discontinued. And Zyman was ecstatic: Crystal Pepsi was effectively neutralized.

"FISH WHERE THE FISH ARE"

Since marketing's primary goal is to enhance profitability, it makes sense to try to increase sales without increasing the expense of getting those sales. One way to do that is to target existing customers. "Concentrate first on the markets that have the most potential—which are usually the markets you are already in—and make sure you are maximizing all of them." Consumers who are already your customers have demonstrated that they have a need for, and the financial resources to buy, your product.

Pursuing additional sales among existing customers is also more cost effective, because you've already achieved some level of brand awareness among your base. You don't need to invest heavily to promote your product, since people are already buying it. And Zyman has even found that "existing markets tend to produce better results than new markets." Convincing people who are already buying your product with some degree of frequency to increase their purchasing is much easier than starting from scratch and encouraging someone to buy the product for the first time.

POSITIONS/IMAGE (handwritten)

POSITION THE COMPETITION

A product's <u>position</u> in the marketplace is what marketers want consumers to think and feel about it. <u>Its image</u>, on the other hand, is the overall impression that consumers have of the product. And when both are the same, marketers have achieved their positioning objective.

A product may be positioned as high end and very expensive, or low end and very cheap, durable, safe, or rich. The key is that marketers are consciously working to get consumers to think a certain way about their product. And if they do a good job, the product's position becomes its image. Just as marketers work to position their own products in certain ways, they can also position the competition. For many years, concedes Zyman, P<u>epsi effectively</u> positioned Coke. Pepsi's "Twice as much for a nickel, too" slogan suggested that Pepsi was a better value. And "The Pepsi Generation" tried to position Coke as the drink for older folk with Pepsi the choice of the youthful. In both cases, Coke was placed on the defensive, having to spend some of its marketing dollars to counter Pepsi's claim, instead of staking out the position the company wanted. Pepsi was in control, to some degree, of Coke's marketing.

By positioning the competition, according to Zyman, you "define the rules of the game in the marketplace." Part of this effort involves defining what should be important to consumers. Pepsi suggested that value should be important in selecting a cola and then shifted to emphasizing taste as the more important consideration with its "Pepsi Challenge" campaign. And by emphasizing taste as the great differentiator, Pepsi suggested to consumers that nothing else was as important as the taste of the cola. If Pepsi had the better-tasting drink, there was no other reason to buy anything else.

What Pepsi marketers did was to narrow how Coke was defined to a single trait in which Pepsi had an advantage—taste—and then broadened their own definition to one of a fun, youthful drink. From this strategy comes a tremendous marketing lesson: As you broaden the definitions of your product, seek to pigeonhole the competition into being defined by one trait, thus helping to boost your product's appeal.

BE WILLING TO CHANGE

To Zyman, the notion that a marketing plan can never be changed is ridiculous: "Experimenting, measuring, and revising are what scientists do to find the best solution. They try things and learn continually in the process." Only by changing your tactics once you learn something new can you improve on your marketing.

Staying wedded to a particular concept or tactic can backfire if market conditions have changed—as they always do. One way to know whether change is needed is to evaluate the results of your current strategy. Are you seeing sales increases? If the answer is no, change is called for. But Zyman encourages change throughout the marketing process and the organization. One example of his belief in the need for change is his having brought more than 125 marketing executives to the company during his tenure, many of whom hailed from outside the beverage industry. Instead of turning to people with the same types of experiences, Zyman sought change via new perspectives and backgrounds.

Changing packaging frequently is also highly recommended. Believing that packaging is "the most under-appreciated marketing tactic," Zyman advocates frequently updating product packaging to ensure that your product stands out from the competition. "This is the loudest possible ad vehicle you have—it's right there in the store when [the customer] is standing there with [his or her] money….This is a place to activate the consumer's impulse to buy." Given the ever-increasing pace of change within society, a company unwilling to take such change into account, and alter its strategies or tactics accordingly, is doomed to failure.

DEVELOP A DIALOGUE WITH YOUR CUSTOMER

Whereas research is a one-way communications effort, a dialogue involves establishing an ongoing sharing of information. Consumer research helps companies map out marketing strategies based on helpful information provided by customers and prospects, but it does little to develop any kind of mutually beneficial relationship. The research participant may go away richer for having been part of a study, but with little else to enhance his or her image of the brand or product being studied.

Developing a dialogue requires getting consumers involved with your brand or product and studying their reactions to changes you suggest. Through a dialogue, you can learn from them what you need to do to improve your product, what you should never change, and what it would take to get them to buy more from you.

The Internet, with its two-way communication capabilities, can help companies establish that dialogue. Information can be both disseminated to customers and collected from them, 24 hours a day.

Keeping in close touch with its customers is something that Coke has not always done well, concedes Zyman. The New Coke launch is proof: Coke's marketers failed to get at the heart of its customers' feelings about the brand and the product. Although research conducted on New Coke told the company that consumers would like a product that tasted sweeter—more like Pepsi—they failed to ask the critical question, "If we took away Coca-Cola and gave you New Coke, would you accept it?" Had they asked that question, they would have learned that customers had an attachment to the product that went well beyond pure taste considerations.

COKE IN THE NEW MILLENNIUM

Under the marketing leadership of Charles Frenette, Coke is dismantling some of the structure introduced by Zyman, including the centralized marketing function. As a former bottler, Frenette sees a need to put responsibility and authority for marketing back in the hands of the bottlers at the local level. While such a move may help achieve some of Zyman's marketing tenets, such as developing a dialogue with customers, it will surely create several different marketing messages, potentially weakening the strength of the Coke brand.

As some of Zyman's strategies are being dismantled, the new Coke CEO, Douglas Daft, is also taking the company in new directions. Recognizing falling demand for carbonated beverages, Coke is planning a major push of its noncarbonated drinks, as well as diversification into new sectors. An early 2000 *Business Week* article reports that Coke's new mission is to dominate the beverage sector, not just the carbonated-beverage market. Given that the market growth of soda is at approximately 2 percent, down from 4 percent in 1998, and juice, tea, and bottled water are growing at 5–28 percent, the company's shift seems well-founded.

Juice-flavored Fruitopia was one of Zyman's responsibilities, while Dasani brand bottled water, Nestea bottled iced tea, and Powerade sports drink came after his departure. All face heavy competition from rival brands, such as Snapple, Arizona, and Lipton Iced Tea, Poland Springs and Evian bottled water, and Gatorade sports drink. Zyman's post-Coke days have been filled with consulting work through his marketing consultancy, Z Group, which works primarily with major consumer products companies.

SERGIO'S MARKETING STRATEGIES

Have a game plan.

Success equals increased sales.

Advertise benefits.

Research, research, research.

Neutralize the competition.

"Fish where the fish are."

Position the competition.

Be willing to change.

Develop a dialogue with your customer.

REFERENCES

"Atlanta Internet firms hire former Coca-Cola marketing executive," by Frances Katz, *Knight-Ridder/Tribune Business News*, August 23, 1999.

"The Aya-Cola speaks, and we can't help but listen," by Patricia Sellers, *Fortune*, July 5, 1999.

"Chasing Sergio," by Karen Benezra and Eleftheria Oarois, *Brandweek*, March 30, 1998.

"Cheat sheet," *Fast Company*, September 1999.

"Coca-Cola: niftiest of the nifty," by Martin Sosnoff, *Forbes*, March 10, 1997.

"The Coke advantage," by Sarah Lorge, *Sales & Marketing Management*, December 1998.

"'Coke is It:' Anxious newspapers hire Coca-Cola marketing guru," by Joe Nicholson, *Editor & Publisher*, May 1, 1999.

"Coke's land of opportunity," *Beverage World*, April 15, 1997.

"Coke's performance gives credibility to the premise that monogamy—and even limited polygamy—between agencies and clients is dead," by Kevin McCormack, *ADWEEK*, March 30, 1998.

"Doug Daft isn't sugarcoating things," *Business Week*, February 7, 2000.

"Experience the real thing," by Jill Rosenfeld, *Fast Company*, January/February 2000.

"Fluid ideas, flowering markets," *Prepared Foods*, January 1997.

"Have a Coke and a smile—please," *Business Week*, August 16, 1999.

"He'd like to teach the world to sell," by Sarah Lorge, *Sales & Marketing Management*, August 1999.

"I'd like to teach the world to sell," by Ellen Neuborne, *Business Week*, June 7, 1999.

"Koonin changes Coke's rules in the marketing game," by Marcy Lamm, *Atlanta Business Chronicle*, April 23, 1999.

"New Coca-Cola marketing plan in the works," *Korea Herald*, October 20, 1999.

"1999 Readers' Choice Awards," by Michael DeLuca, *Restaurant Hospitality*, July 1999.

"Now, Coke is no longer 'it,'" *Business Week*, February 28, 2000.

"Sergio Zyman, the outspoken former Coca-Cola marketing guru has news that some on Madison Avenue won't want to hear: Traditional marketing is dead," by Scott Donaton, *Advertising Age*, May 31, 1999.

"So he quit, so what?" by Betsy Morris, *Fortune*, April 13, 1998.

"Will Coke take local route?" by Lisa Campbell, *Marketing*, March 26, 1998.

Part Two

GURU THINKERS

CHAPTER SIX

INFORMATION AGE MARKETER

Seth Godin

Marketing in an interactive world is a collaborative activity—with the marketer helping the consumer to buy and the consumer helping the marketer to sell.

—Don Peppers, coauthor,
The One to One Future

INTRODUCTION

Great ideas are dangerous, claims Seth Godin. In fact, ideas can cause normally intelligent business people to stupidly invest their life savings on concepts that just won't fly. And yet, Godin has had a lot of great ideas, several of which have helped him start and run a successful publishing company, an Internet direct-marketing firm, and several smaller ventures during his high school and college days. His most recent idea, and book by the same name, *Permission Marketing*, has virtually become a marketing movement.

Permission marketing—not to be confused with email marketing, he warns—involves rewarding people for their attention to your marketing efforts in order to develop such a level of trust and rapport that you allow purchases to become automatic. Offline examples of permission marketing have existed for decades, in the form of the automatically delivered coffee or water cooler service, for example. But Godin is the first to lay out a method of applying those principles in the digital arena.

Godin's concept has been adopted quickly, perhaps because the process of permission marketing rolls into one several already popular approaches—one-to-one marketing, guerrilla marketing, and email marketing. The personalization of one-to-one marketing generally results in higher sales and revenue, guerrilla marketing uses unconventional means to capture the attention of consumers, and email marketing provides a cost-effective means of carrying out both types of programs.

GODIN GROWS UP

In the last decade, Godin has risen from publishing company owner to direct-marketing guru. After gaining prominence following the highly successful publication of *The Beardstown Ladies Investment Guide*, which his firm packaged, he went on to further notoriety through his collaborations with Jay Conrad Levinson, whose *Guerrilla Marketing Handbook* and *Guerrilla Marketing for the Home-Based Business* were both published with Godin's help.

But Godin's official jump from publishing occurred in 1995 with the establishment of Yoyodyne Entertainment, an Internet direct-marketing company. Taking what he had learned about small-business marketing and combining it with his understanding of the online world, he created a new electronic-business model. Just a few years later, the company was sold to Yahoo! for $29.6 million.

The objective of Yoyodyne was to combine fun and entertainment with direct marketing on the Internet. Major corporations like American Express and Microsoft retained the firm to create elaborate sweepstakes and games to drive traffic to their Web site. Others quickly became believers after seeing the stunning results that are possible: a better response to advertisements with a lower total cost. Part of that advantage comes compliments of the Internet.

THE BASICS OF PERMISSION MARKETING

Permission marketing is really a method for overcoming the clutter of mass marketing that is reducing consumers' response to advertising messages. Because consumers are now exposed to more than 2000 commercial messages a day, says Godin—from TV, radio, magazines, newspapers, billboards, sides of buses, and the Internet, few people remember even one commercial they saw the day before. That's disheartening for marketers who spend millions to encourage consumers—and businesses—to buy their products or services. Godin recognized this quandary and developed a better way to market: Get consumers to consent to pay attention to the messages marketers want to get across. Permission marketing is that alternative approach.

The first step in the process of getting permission is to build a Web site for people to visit. Once they are there, the challenge is starting a dialogue with them. Work to find out all you can about them and their needs. Godin suggests asking "Hi, who are you?" to start.

"One way to sell a customer something in the future is simply to get his or her permission in advance. You'll do this by engaging the customer in a dialogue—an interactive relationship with you and the customer participating," he explains. So instead of interrupting someone's busy life with an irrelevant advertising message, such as through a TV commercial, direct-mail letter, or phone call, first try and involve that person in the selling process.

In return for their commitment to pay more attention to advertising messages, however, marketers need to be prepared to reward consumers for their time. With permission marketing, consumers agree essentially to actively participate in a marketing campaign, virtually guaranteeing that the response to such a campaign will be drastically better than that to the traditional direct-marketing approach. Godin throws out the suggestion that a 70 percent response is possible when the message is relevant, compared with the standard 1–2 percent direct-mail response rate. The biggest difference, he argues, is that permission marketing is anticipated, personal, and relevant, as opposed to traditional direct marketing, which is none of these. Permission marketing is anticipated because the consumer has agreed to receive messages from marketers, and when the messages turn out to be interesting and fun, they can be eagerly awaited. It is *personal* in that each message is directed specifically to a particular individual, by name. And it is *relevant* in that the marketing information involves something the consumer is personally interested in.Godin describes the process of permission marketing as one of "turning strangers into friends and friends into customers." It's about establishing a long-term, ongoing relationship that will be increasingly profitable as more and more information is shared. The more information the consumer is willing to share, the better the job the marketer can do to meet the consumer's needs economically. The result is more purchases by the consumer, more revenue for the marketer, and feedback regarding which products and services are relevant to the consumer.

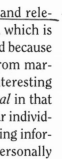

Done well, permission marketing can be an example of Jesse Berst's spiral-marketing concept: Consumers buy more and provide more personal information to businesses on the Web that can best meet their needs, thus improving the company's understanding of those needs and enabling it to sell more to the consumer. The more information that is shared along the way, the stronger will be the bond established between customer and marketer. And what makes that process possible is the interactivity of the Internet.

USE INTERACTIVE TECHNOLOGY TO BOND WITH CUSTOMERS

Although permission marketing predates the Internet, allows Godin, the power and reach of the Web has brought the costs of permission marketing down considerably. The interactive and communication capabilities the Internet provides make it possible to contact millions of prospects online at virtually no cost, as well as—and more importantly—enabling a true dialogue to take place between marketer and consumer. No longer is there simply one-way communication, from marketer to consumer. Through Web sites, email, and online chats and discussions, consumers can respond to inquiries and provide valuable feedback.

The process of getting to know your prospects and turning them into customers involves five basic steps, says Godin. He considers "getting to know" your prospects a lot like dating: Each person shares information—tentatively at first—with the hope that, over time, a serious relationship will develop. Permission marketing follows the same rules in trying to get to know customers. By winnowing down the potential pool of prospects to only those whose needs fit the company's offerings, the marketer increases the success rate of developing a serious relationship with the customer.

"Interruption" marketers, in contrast, eschew dating in favor of trying to instantly marry each prospect; the result is that very few accept the marriage proposal, and the marketer has to move on to try to woo the next prospect. Not only is this approach time consuming, but it's also quite costly, not to mention prone to failure.

The first step in gaining permission is to offer an incentive for paying attention to the company's marketing message. Prospects need to have a good enough reason to pay attention and break away from the many other ways they have to spend their time. Godin's company, Yoyodyne, frequently used sweepstakes as an incentive to participate. Each time a prospect agreed to pay attention to an advertisement, he or she received a chance to win a prize. And when the amount of money at stake is $100,000 or more, it's not too tough to get people interested in participating. After offering an incentive and getting the prospect to buy into the process, the second step in permission marketing is to begin to provide information —a "curriculum over time"—that teaches the consumer about the company's products or services. And since the person has agreed up front to pay attention to the information, it's much easier to teach him or her about the products and services available. In addition, because the company doesn't have to worry about devising tactics to hold the person's attention, such as an eye-catching layout or entertaining music, the message can be highly focused on the benefits of the product. The consumer learns specific ways that that particular product or service can satisfy his or her needs. The message is very personal.

As the allure of the incentive will begin to wear off over time, the third step involves reinforcing the initial incentive. This means adjusting the incentive to better fit the prospect, such as adding more chances to win the sweepstakes or giving the option to select a different prize to those less interested in winning money. After reinforcing the incentive, the next step is to increase the level of permission received from the prospect. "The goal is to motivate the consumer to give more and more permission over time," explains Godin, "permission to gather more data about the customer's personal life, hobbies, or interests," which the company can then use to customize its product and service offerings.

Once the relationship has been established, an incentive given to continue that relationship, and permission granted to both give and receive marketing information, the next step is to leverage that permission to sell more products and services. Using the increasingly valuable personal information offered by the prospect, companies can determine the most effective way of marketing to that individual—and then do it, repeatedly. And since the products and services are truly relevant and useful to that individual, the bond that has developed is long-lasting and beneficial to both parties, like a marriage that only gets better with time.

The process of information sharing is facilitated by the capabilities of the Internet. Surveys can be sent and completed online, questions asked and answered via email, and discussions held online, all of which make it possible to strike up a meaningful customer relationship.

SIMPLIFY YOUR WEB SITE

Making contact with potential customers is the first order of business for permission marketers, who rely on a Web site to achieve that goal. In the digital era, a company's Web site is the equivalent of Grand Central Station—a place where companies and individuals connect. But a Web site doesn't have to be difficult to get around in—or at least, it shouldn't be. Godin suggests that to be most effective, Web sites should be no more than three pages long.

Visitors head to a company's Web site for a number of reasons. In some cases, they may want to learn something, such as finding a recipe. In other cases, they may be there specifically to buy something, such as office supplies, or they may have come for entertainment, such as downloading an MP3 file or scoping out how the stock market is performing at that hour. In all cases, it's the marketer's responsibility to make the site as inviting and easy to use as possible. Doing so can yield more satisfied customers and higher sales, reports a *CIO* article: "Making goal-directed visitors happy means streamlining your site, reducing the number of pages or clicks used. In effect, it means shortening the distance between customers and the cash register."

Making a Web site easier to navigate also enhances a visitor's opinion of the company, which helps to build a relationship—the goal of permission marketing. The simpler the site, the easier it is for visitors to accomplish what they sought to accomplish there in the first place, whether it's locating technical information, applying for a loan, or purchasing a product. "Sites that do a better job of understanding and catering to individual users naturally provide higher levels of satisfaction" reports *CIO*.

Godin recommends that, in order to cater to individual information needs, companies have two Web sites: one for customers and one for prospects. One site doesn't fit all, he argues. "Current customers need a totally different kind of experience. The need to be able to go online and find out where in the factory their order is….Someone who hasn't been a customer yet doesn't want to know any of that stuff. They just want to know if they should become a customer and how?" Creating a site for a particular type of user's needs achieves two objectives: It keeps the site simple, and it allows the content to be extremely relevant.

REWARD CONSUMERS FOR THEIR TIME

"Infoglut," "interruption marketing," and "incentive" are the three I's at the core of Godin's "permission marketing" concept. Because of today's abundance of information, consumers are overwhelmed —both by ads competing for their attention and everything else in their lives. The result is that incentives are required in order to gain a person's agreement to pay attention to a particular marketing message. These incentives can take the form of information that is of interest to the consumer, or entertainment, such as participation in a game or sweepstakes—preferably with a large prize—or an outright payment. Securing "volunteers" costs money one way or another. But Yoyodyne's model *guarantees* a certain number of volunteers —something traditional direct-mail marketers simply can't do.

One 1999 Yoyodyne promotion, called EZWheels, lasted nine weeks and gave participants the chance to win $20,000 toward the car of their choice. Sponsors of the promotion paid a little more than $2 per participant for a guarantee of at least 25,000 volunteers. In contrast, points out Godin, automakers typically spend between $.60 and $1.00 to send one piece of direct mail to a prospect—and that prospect hasn't even indicated a willingness to review the information! At least EZWheels sponsors know that sweepstakes participants are reading and considering their promotional material.

During the promotion, Yoyodyne collected information on the contestants' email addresses, home zip codes, make and models of the car they currently own, and when they plan to buy their next car. This last piece of data is critical for determining how serious each contestant is about buying a new car. Then, each week for nine weeks, participants were sent an email message inviting them to visit a section of the automaker's site to learn about a new car feature, in return for another contest entry.

A similar program organized for American Express, called EZSpree, offered customers who shopped at certain EZSpree merchants a chance to win an online shopping spree. The results demonstrated the strength of this marketing model: Thirty-five percent of contestants clicked through to sponsoring merchant sites, with Wal-Mart's site selling $1000 worth of Barbie dolls to participants.

The incentive doesn't have to be money (although money is generally valued by most consumers), but it does need to be of enough interest that prospects would be willing to trade their valuable time to receive it. Or in the case of sweepstakes, it needs to be valuable enough that prospects would trade their time for a *chance* to receive it.

GIVE PROMOTIONAL CONTROL BACK TO THE CONSUMER

Americans are becoming more concerned about public access to their private information on the Internet, says a recent *Marketing* article. In fact, 8 out of 10 consumers believe that they have lost control over how companies collect and use their personal data. Obviously, this fear affects consumers' willingness to share personal information and can sabotage marketers' efforts to learn more about potential customers. Fortunately, permission marketing gives marketers a way to bolster consumers' confidence and feelings of security.

To make the most of the permission that consumers give to receive advertisements, companies need to offer an "explicit bargain," a term Don Peppers, of Peppers and Rogers fame, uses in reference to situations in which individuals know up front what they are getting into in the way of agreeing to pay attention to advertising information. In return for something of value, they give their permission to be marketed to. The key is that, in return for the incentive, prospects know exactly how the information they provide will be used. If there is any question about whether the information will be shared with other companies or made public in some way, permission will not be granted. Web sites should explicitly state who has access to the personal information provided by the prospect. Allaying their fears that their private data will become public increases the level of permission granted and strengthens trust toward the marketer. Then, instead of viewing a company as a potential threat to privacy, prospects can start see it as a protector. Of course, the marketer should make sure that all privacy policies are clearly and vehemently stated.

AIM TO SELL BY SUBSCRIPTION

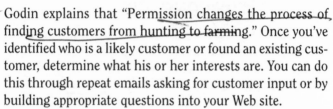

Godin explains that "Permission changes the process of finding customers from hunting to farming." Once you've identified who is a likely customer or found an existing customer, determine what his or her interests are. You can do this through repeat emails asking for customer input or by building appropriate questions into your Web site.

An excellent example of building in subscription opportunities is at Amazon.com. Each visitor to the site is invited to specify book and music topics, authors, or musicians that are of interest to him or her in return for advance information about new products. Amazon asks for permission to recontact the person with the kind of information that is specified and then distributes a customized email message when such products are released. By sending an email with information specific to that individual's interest, marketers easily cut through the clutter of other promotional programs and continue to build a bond with the customer. They also create buying opportunities that can be worth millions of dollars. At least that's what Amazon discovered early on. With just one broadcast email to customers, Amazon.com sold 12 million books, for example. Total cost to distribute the message? $0. Look at those profit margins!

But there are several levels of permission, with each one indicating a higher level of trust on the part of the consumer and profits on the part of the marketer. The first and lowest level of permission is situational permission. This level is initiated by the consumer and is specified to be effective over a finite time period. When a consumer calls a customer service department, for example, there is permission to ask for information in order to better assist the prospect. However, when the caller hangs up, that permission ends.

The second level of permission—brand trust—results from a consumer's familiarity with, and confidence in, a particular brand. As Godin puts it, "Brand trust is a vague, but soft and safe form of product confidence that consumers feel when interacting with a brand that's spent a ton of money on consistent, frequent interruptive messages." Although this is the level of permission that most marketers aspire to, it is extremely expensive to achieve and maintain. It also takes a long time to develop and can be destroyed with one bad move, such as a product extension that falls flat.

Setting your standards higher makes a lot more sense. The third level, personal relationship, relies on the relationship you already have with an individual to determine whether he or she will give more permission. Godin believes that this level is the "most powerful form of permission for making major shifts in a consumer's behavior. It is also the single easiest way to move someone to an intravenous level of permission" (the highest level there is). This level is based on the premise that it's much easier to sell more products to someone who has already bought from you, rather than trying to build a relationship with a new customer.

Above personal relationships, is the points permission level. Points are a method of attracting and keeping a prospect's attention by offering a scalable approach to rewarding them; that is, prospects can collect points that can be redeemed for something of value. S&H Green Stamps are a perfect example, says Godin. Every time you made a purchase from a participating store, you received a number of green stamps in direct proportion to how much you spent. Fill a booklet with stamps, and you were eligible to redeem it for certain rewards. But there are actually two types of points programs: point liability and point chance. With point liability programs, there is an actual cost for each point given to consumers. Airline frequent flyer programs are a good example of this, and the fact that they have to carry a liability on their balance sheet equal to the number of unredeemed frequent flyer miles is proof that there is real value.

The point chance model enables prospects to earn more chances to win a big prize, rather than being given a specified number of points with a set value. The advantage of this model is that since the value of the prize is fixed—at, say, $100,000—then one more point distributed to prospects costs nothing extra. But keeping prospects involved is harder and requires the marketer to create a series of interactions, including events and promotions, to improve a prospect's odds of winning.

At the pinnacle of permission marketing is the "intravenous" level of permission, in which the marketer has the consent of the prospect to make buying decisions on his or her behalf. Automatic replenishment of supplies is one example of this level: The customer relies on a supplier to ensure that a product is never depleted. Until the customer says stop, the marketer has his or her continued permission to make deliveries of specified products or services. A variation of this level of permission is purchase on approval, wherein a second authorization is required before the customer is billed. With this "negative option," participants in book clubs, for instance, always have the option not to have a particular book shipped the following month. In other words, they can opt out of receiving the book. But those who don't opt out will automatically have the volume arrive on their doorstep as the selection of the month.

Permission marketers obviously want to reach this

highest level, because if they do, they have earned the trust of their customer, as well as the responsibility to continue to provide products and services that are desired. One wrong guess and the permission may end. However, the reward of guessing correctly is that sales increase, along with profits, as customers buy more.

MAKE ADVERTISING FUN AGAIN

Since we all know we're being marketed to, why not make it a game? Literally. That's the basic thinking behind Godin's revolutionary idea. Although permission marketing itself is not predicated on playing games and having fun, fun is one thing consumers are having less of, which is probably why sweepstakes, games, and contests on the Internet are some of the most popular activities. People want a break. So when permission marketers link fun and games with marketing, consumers are willing to participate. In return for a chance to win a new car, prospects might need to read relevant articles and view certain online ads, for example. The more articles read and the more ads scanned, the more chances of winning that person earns. Without the possibility of a prize, few consumers would bother to spend time looking at ads. It's the game that makes participation worthwhile. And it's the game that is helping permission marketers to achieve stunning response rates, for less money than traditional direct-marketing programs cost.

With so many images forced on consumers every day, getting them involved is one of the few ways to make an ad stand out. Interactivity is a weapon that permission marketers build into each campaign. And it works, as Godin has shown.

THE FUTURE OF PERMISSION MARKETING

Despite the fact that Yahoo! bought Yoyodyne for close to $30 million in 1998, just three years after its formation, the concept of making game playing and contests part of the marketing process will surely live on. In fact, Yoyodyne has become Yahoo's direct-marketing arm, available to assist corporations in applying the basic tenets of permission marketing. The company's database of consumers and its services will be integrated into Yahoo's banner ads, promotions, and merchandising to reach out to the 40 million-plus monthly visitors to Yahoo and the 25 million My Yahoo members.

SETH'S INTERNET MARKETING STRATEGIES
Use interactive technology to bond with customers.
Simplify your Web site.
Reward consumers for their time.
Give promotional control back to the consumer.
Aim to sell by subscription.
Make advertising fun again.

REFERENCES

"Bausch & Lomb sees Yoyodyne's Web vision," by Adrienne Mand, *ADWEEK*, May 11, 1998.

The Booststrapper's Bible, by Seth Godin, Upstart Publishing Company, 1998.

"Card briefs," *American Banker*, July 27, 1998.

"Consumers can call the shots in ad relationships," by Laura Mazur, *Marketing*, April 8, 1999.

"Future sales: Get the customer's permission first, then make your pitch," by Robert Mendenhall, *Business Marketing*, June 1, 1999.

"Goals, permission lead to site payoff," by Dana Blankenhorn, *Business Marketing*, September 1, 1999.

"'Permission: a key to online success," by Janet Herlihy, *HFN*, October 18, 1999.

Permission Marketing, by Seth Godin, Simon & Schuster, 1999.

"Permission marketing: the way to make advertising work again," *Direct Marketing*, May 1999.

"Pipeline announced," *InfoWorld*, October 19, 1998.

"Seth Godin: Feeding the gorilla," *CIO*, August 1, 1999.

"$20,000 Web prize offer collects key buyer data," by Patricia Riedman, *Automotive News*, December 15, 1997.

CHAPTER SEVEN

MARKETING PROFESSOR

Philip Kotler

Today most markets are characterized by an abundance of suppliers and brands. There is a shortage of customers, not products.
—Philip Kotler

INTRODUCTION

It could be said that Philip Kotler wrote the book on marketing. In fact, he did. His *Marketing Management* textbook is the standard marketing text used throughout the country—and probably the world—for graduate marketing classes. In its eighth edition, *Marketing Management* is proof of the enduring value of Kotler's teaching and his systematic approach. *Principles of Marketing*, another ubiquitous Kotler text, is used at universities worldwide.

Kotler's most recent book, *Kotler on Marketing: How to Create, Win, and Dominate Markets*, is essentially a summary of his other marketing texts, written for managers rather than students. And it has received rave reviews, much like his other books, which have sold in excess of 3,000,000 copies in 20 languages. In the book, Kotler outlines strategies that forward-thinking companies should use to create and sustain a competitive advantage in future markets. These strategies are born out of some predictions that he makes for marketing in 2005, which include substantially increased outsourcing, reduced TV advertising (to be replaced by specialized online media), complex proprietary customer databases containing detailed information on customer preferences, and a breakdown of the wholesale–retail distribution relationship, primarily because of customers' increased access to, and use of, the Internet to make needed purchases—both *in business-to-consumer* (B2C) and *business-to-business* (B2B) markets.

Kotler has long been the marketing master, helping students of the subject understand how to determine where their company is, where it should be headed, and how it can reasonably get there.

PHILIP THE PIONEER

The S.C. Johnson & Son Distinguished Professor of International Marketing at Northwestern University's J.L. Kellogg Graduate School of Management, Kotler introduced some of the basic approaches to marketing strategy and marketing analysis. His marketing career spans 38 years, beginning with an associate professorship of economics at Roosevelt University and shifting to an assistant professorship at Northwestern in 1962.

His first marketing text was published in 1969, two years after he was named professor of marketing at Northwestern. Since then, he has influenced tens of thousands—if not hundreds of thousands—of marketing minds through his teaching and writing. He has written a total of nine books and has several in the works. His consulting clients have included major international corporations, such as IBM, General Electric, AT&T, Merck, and Bank of America. Kotler earned an MA from the University of Chicago after attending DePaul University briefly. He received a PhD from MIT and completed postdoctoral study at Harvard.

One of Kotler's contributions to the field of marketing has been to view a company, its products, and its services as part of a larger system. Perhaps his economic background and training influenced his thinking in this regard, which advocates beginning any marketing program with a complete analysis of a company's position in the marketplace and then developing a multifaceted campaign to communicate effectively with target markets. Kotler's core teachings include the marketing strategies in this chapter.

PREPARE A COMPLETE MARKETING PLAN

One of Kotler's strengths as a marketer and educator is his ability to analyze and connect seemingly disparate events and concepts. "Marketing managers, in order to make better marketing decisions, needed to analyze markets and competition in systems terms, explicating the forces at work and their various interdependencies," he says. Perhaps that's why his approach to developing a marketing plan includes preparing an internal and external market analysis first. Called a *situation analysis,* this initial evaluation of internal and external market forces helps marketers see where the market is headed and where a particular company's opportunities lie. A situation analysis contains four main components: a description of the current situation facing the company; an analysis of the company's *s*trengths, *w*eaknesses, *o*pportunities, and *t*hreats (also called a SWOT analysis); an assessment of the main issues facing the business; and the basic assumptions being made about the future.

An analysis of the company's situation should contain a statistical picture of the company's performance for the last three to five years, examining sales, market share, prices, costs, and profits, as well as the performance of main competitors. In a SWOT analysis, an evaluation of the company's strengths and weaknesses is an internal assessment, whereas a look at opportunities and threats is an external assessment.

Start with a list of five major opportunities that offer a "high return and a high probability of success," followed with a list of five significant threats that the company may have to deal with. By identifying potential threats, the company will be in a much better position to deal with them should they arise.

Using the list, the business can then analyze its strengths and weaknesses relative to its opportunities and threats. "Every company must decide which strengths need to be further improved, and which weaknesses must be corrected, based on the looming opportunities and threats," says Kotler.

The next area to be examined comprises the main issues facing the business. By listing approximately five such issues, the company can begin to plan how to address them. For example, how do your company's costs compare with your competition's? Is your company ahead or behind in the development of an Internet presence? Are you facing comparatively high employee or customer turnover? All of these questions represent critical business issues that need to be addressed.

Finally, your situation analysis should have a list of main assumptions about the future. For instance, what do you expect your market share gains to be this year? Will inflation be an issue in the next year or two? How will competitors respond to any losses in market share? Will they reduce their prices? Is there pending legislation that can affect the company or the industry? After assessing your company's current situation, you are in a much better position to lay out a strategy for marketing the company's products and services. It makes sense that you should first know where you are and what your objectives are before determining the best way to reach your goals. That's exactly what a situation analysis helps companies to do. The situation analysis then becomes the first part of a complete marketing plan, according to Kotler. Other important sections are marketing objectives and goals, marketing strategy, the marketing action plan, and marketing controls.

Objectives are broad targets to be achieved in the next year or in the next evaluation period. They might include increasing customer satisfaction, increasing sales, and reducing employee turnover. Goals, on the other hand, are the measurable components of these broad objectives, such as increasing customer satisfaction by 20 percent or reducing employee turnover by 10 percent.The marketing strategy then results from these goals and objectives and may be described along six lines, says Kotler:

- *The Target Market.* Divide your target market into three groups: the primary, secondary, and tertiary markets, or those who are ready and able to buy; those who are able, but less ready and willing; and those who are willing, but not yet able.

- *Core Positioning.* Find the core idea or benefit on which to base your offering. (Volvo's core positioning centers on safety, for instance.)

- *Price Positioning.* Determine how to price your offerings relative to your core benefit.

- *Total Value Proposition.* Decide how to best answer the question "Why should I buy from you?" through your combination of features, benefits, and price.

- *Distribution Strategy.* Determine how to continue to get your offerings into your prospects' and customers' hands.

- *Communication Strategy.* Determine how the marketing budget should be allocated to reach the target market(s), using all the available marketing tactics.

Following the strategy development, an action plan should be drafted that identifies who is responsible for which key tasks and that sets completion dates. And finally, a control mechanism needs to be implemented that builds in a regular review of goals and objectives achieved, such as a quarterly or monthly review.

COLLABORATE WITH CUSTOMERS

Codesigning products and services with the help of customer input achieves a pair of objectives: (1) creating products that customers want and will buy and (2) demonstrating how important customer needs are to your company. Since so many customers choose to do business elsewhere due to business apathy, anything you do to prove how important the customer is to your company can only strengthen the bond between the two of you.

One way to shift the focus to customer needs and away from company interests is to add the "four C's" (which stand for *customer value, cost to the customer, convenience, and communication*) to the traditional "four P's" of marketing (*product, price, promotion, and place*), since the four P's take the seller's view rather than the buyer's. Kotler argues, "While marketers see themselves as selling a product, customers see themselves as buying value or a solution to a problem."

He also sees the need for two more P's—politics and public opinion—because marketers may want to use political lobbying to affect market demand, and public opinion can quickly shift interest to, and away from, certain products and services. In fact, getting customers interested and involved in assisting companies to improve their products is becoming more and more common. Magazines are setting up reader advisory boards, for example, to collect ongoing feedback and ideas from subscribers regarding their interests in, and reaction to, the publication's editorial direction. In doing so, they improve the quality of the product and strengthen reader loyalty.

In many cases, customers are more than willing to share their opinions and insights. Customer satisfaction surveys have been around for some time now and are excellent tools for learning how well your company is meeting customer needs. Taking the process one step further requires the company to apply the knowledge gained from customers to refining current products and developing new ones. Offering existing customers the option to purchase new products they helped to create can build a solid base before the product is even introduced to the mass market. And it can turn those existing customers into strong advocates for the company, working to convert prospects into new customers. Once a sale has occurred, the trick to increased profitability is to retain and build that customer relationship.

FOCUS ON CUSTOMER RETENTION

According to Kotler, "Marketing is defined as the science and art of finding, keeping, and growing profitable customers. Today's companies are shifting their emphasis from finding customers to learning how to keep and grow them."

"Customer care," Kotler argues, is significantly more profitable than customer acquisition. This makes perfect sense when you know that the cost of acquiring a new customer can reach into the thousands of dollars. And attracting a new customer is "five times the cost of keeping a current customer," says Kotler, which makes it obvious why serving existing customers is much less costly. In fact, just pursuing new business is expensive—the total cost of a single sales call is in the neighborhood of $500 for many companies. Multiply that by the size of your target market, and you may be out of business soon.

Research by another marketing professor, Adrian Payne, of the Cranfield School of Management, bears out Kotler's assertion. Payne's research indicates that 80 percent of all companies spend too much on customer acquisition and not enough on customer retention. The investment can pay off handsomely, however: As little as a 5 percent increase in retention can produce a 35–150 percent increase in profitability.

Much more important, though, is the lifetime value of a customer. "Companies have discovered that the longer that customers stay with a company, the more profitable they are," says Kotler. This is the result of four major factors:

- Retained customers buy more over time through cross-selling and upselling if they are satisfied with the company's products and services.

- The cost of serving a customer declines over time because "transactions become routinized," reducing the need for large investments of time and paperwork.

- Highly satisfied customers recommend the seller to other potential buyers, who then increase the profitability of that initial customer.

- Long-term customers are less sensitive to reasonable price increases introduced by the seller, thus maintaining and even improving profits realized by that customer.

The key phrase at the heart of this situation is a "highly satisfied" customer. Kotler states that customers can expe-

rience one of five levels of satisfaction, with "highly satisfied" being the best a company can hope for. "Satisfied,"
"indifferent," "dissatisfied," and "very dissatisfied," are not
good enough to solidify a long-term, profitable relationship
with a customer, making the aforementioned four factors
moot. Without a high level of satisfaction, it is unlikely that
a customer is going to buy more from you, much less suggest that friends and colleagues should also do business
with you. "The probability that the new customer will buy
again is strongly related to his level of satisfaction with the
first purchase," says Kotler.

But don't despair if you think that customer satisfaction
levels could be higher at your business. Customers who are
dissatisfied can become some of your staunchest support-
ers if they are encouraged to reveal the reason for their dissatisfaction. Why is that? Because you are then given the
opportunity to correct the situation and impress the customer with your responsiveness and concern for his or her
well-being. "Ironically," Kotler says, "customers whose
complaints are satisfactorily resolved often become more
loyal than customers who were never dissatisfied."

A word to the wise, however: A dissatisfied customer
whose problem is not resolved is likely to tell an average of
11 others about his or her negative experience with your
company. Moreover, your biggest challenge is identifying
who these customers are. That's because only 5 percent of
dissatisfied customers will ever speak up, and, unfortunately,
your customers are dissatisfied with their purchases about
25 percent of the time. The main reason for this lack of communication is that customers generally don't know how to
complain or whom to complain to, which means that one
solution is to make it obvious and easy for customers to
express displeasure with any part of their experience with
your company. Advertising your toll-free phone numbers for
comments, providing postpaid response cards during a pur-

chase, and mailing postpurchase surveys are just some of the approaches used by U.S. companies to encourage feedback.

The message is clear: Unless you begin work to keep—rather than find—customers, you may soon be facing an uphill marketing battle. According to Kotler, "As more companies master the art of satisfying and retaining customers, it will become increasingly hard for companies to attract new customers through getting them to switch. That forces still more companies to master the art of creating loyal customers."

PURSUE A SUSTAINABLE COMPETITIVE ADVANTAGE

Delivering more value than your competitors is one way to build and strengthen long-term customer relationships, thereby improving customer retention and profitability. The three primary ways to gain a competitive advantage, says Michael Porter in *Competitive Strategy*, are:

- Charging a lower price

- Helping customers reduce costs in other areas of their business

- Offering more benefits for the same money

However, companies that continue to use "Neanderthal marketing" tactics, says Kotler, will find themselves quickly losing any competitive advantage they may once have had. Neanderthal practices are those that Kotler considers obsolete, including the following:

- Equating marketing with selling

- Emphasizing customer acquisition, rather than customer care

- Trying to make a profit on each transaction, rather than trying to profit by managing the customer's lifetime value

- Pricing based on marking up cost, rather than target pricing

- Planning each communication tool separately, rather than integrating marketing communication tools

- Selling the product, rather than trying to understand and meet the customer's real needs

In the new era of cyber- and one-to-one marketing, companies will need to leave behind these internally focused strategies in place of more customer-oriented messages in order to sustain any kind of competitive advantage. Businesses that attempt to continue marketing as before will be left behind by competitors that are better able to meet customers' needs.

INTEGRATE MARKETING TACTICS

Instead of treating each promotional tool, such as advertising, public relations, sales promotion, direct mail, and sponsorships, as a separate marketing activity, Kotler strongly advocates coordinating the selection and implementation of all of these activities to gain the best overall promotional results. He points out that companies which do not integrate all of their marketing tactics may run into problems: "Not only may they end up using these promotional tools in the wrong proportions, but they may also fail to create and deliver a consistent message with different tools." Too often, however, the success or failure of a promotional campaign rests on one tool—generally advertising—instead of a mix of elements. A better approach would be to use advertising as the first step in a phased marketing communications program, followed by a series of other tools. The introduction of a new product, for instance, might first be announced by a national TV ad push and then followed by a direct mailing to a target prospect base, complemented by a publicity campaign through print publications and a sweepstakes at the corporate Web site, which is mentioned in all other parts of the program. Working together, the program's communications components can achieve better results than any one individual tool working alone. And given the rising cost of advertising, many companies do not have adequate marketing budgets to sustain a significant advertising campaign that can make an impact.

To integrate marketing communications, Kotler says, companies must recognize "all contact points where the customer may encounter the company, its products, and its brands. Each brand contact will deliver a message, either good, bad, or indifferent. The company must strive to deliver a consistent and positive message at all contact points." That means that, in addition to integrating all communications efforts, all four of the earlier mentioned P's must be integrated: product, price, promotion, and place of sale. "The company cannot charge a high price for a poor-quality product or charge a high price for a good-quality product but provide poor service," for example, says Kotler. Each "P" must support and complement the others in order to achieve the best possible results from a marketing program.

MAKE SURE MARKETING COMES BEFORE SELLING

Many people equate marketing with selling, believing that the two are identical. In fact, they are two separate processes, and indeed, selling begins where marketing leaves off. This insight can completely change a marketing organization, affecting who has decision-making power, who gets promoted (many companies routinely promote sales representatives into marketing management positions, thinking that one is good training for the other), how budgets are allocated, and which tools are selected as part of a marketing plan.

Marketing involves everything you do to persuade someone to buy your product or service, and selling is simply the transaction that occurs following a successful marketing campaign. But make no mistake; they are not one and the same. Peter Drucker stated that "the aim of marketing is to make selling superfluous," meaning that when marketing is successful at discovering customers' needs and delivering satisfying solutions, no selling is necessary. Unfortunately, such situations are rare.

Kotler gives a few examples of companies that believed, erroneously, that selling and marketing were essentially the same—that customers would buy whatever they were presented with, no matter what the marketing message was. Levi's and The Body Shop are two examples that stopped marketing and focused on selling, to their detriment, according to Kotler. In the meantime, competitors moved in with copycat products that consumers liked just as well and could buy for less.

"Marketing is the homework that managers undertake to assess needs, measure their extent and intensity, and determine whether a profitable opportunity exists....Marketing continues throughout the product's life, trying to find new customers, improve product appeal and performance, learn from product sales results, and manage repeat sales," explains Kotler.

When marketing is managed properly, a company develops new products in response to stated or observed customer needs, and customers love what is offered and buy heavily. At the same time, the customers encourage their friends to do likewise. All of the actions and reactions provide feedback to the company to help it develop more and better follow-on products.

Part of the key to success is a marketing mindset that exists throughout the company, from research and development, to manufacturing, to human resources, to purchasing, to marketing, and on and on. Successful marketers place responsibility for marketing throughout the organization, expecting everyone to assist in serving customers.

KOTLER'S NEXT MOVE

Given Kotler's long-standing history at Northwestern and his impressive track record of groundbreaking marketing books, don't expect much to change in the future. His upcoming books will most likely take a look at marketing strategies in use around the world, as well as the increasing impact of the Internet on marketing. He will most likely continue to lecture and speak globally to corporate and institutional audiences, spreading his marketing management message.

KOTLER'S MARKETING PRIMER
Prepare a complete marketing plan.
Collaborate with customers.
Focus on customer retention.
Integrate marketing tactics.
Make sure marketing comes before selling.

REFERENCES

"Kotler on marketing," by Littleton Maxwell, *Library Journal*, April 1, 1999.

"Kotler on marketing," by Michael Obermire, *Across the Board*, May 1999.

Kotler on Marketing, by Philip Kotler, The Free Press, 1999.

"Kotler on marketing," *Publishers Weekly*, March 1, 1999.

"Kotler's latest rich in information," by Robert Mendenhall, *Business Marketing*, December 1, 1999.

"Other titles of interest," *Latin Trade*, September 1999.

"Out-dated ideas need to remain in the Stone Age," by Laura Mazur, *Marketing*, June 24, 1999.

CHAPTER EIGHT

GUERRILLA GURU

Jay Conrad Levinson

Guerrilla tactics...provide you with an alternative to standard expensive marketing. They enable you to increase your sales with a minimum of expense and a maximum of smarts.

—Jay Conrad Levinson

INTRODUCTION

The man who coined the now common phrase "guerrilla marketing," Jay Conrad Levinson, began a small-business revolution in 1983 with the publication of his first book, by the same title. *Guerrilla Marketing* has inspired many small-business owners to think differently about how they approach marketing and sales; the book provides plenty of examples regarding how lean-and-mean companies can best their larger rivals when armed with the proper strategy.

Guerrilla Marketing's premise is that smaller businesses have competitive advantages that they need to leverage and exploit in order to beat out larger companies for business. Without multimillion dollar marketing budgets, small businesses need to apply innovative and inexpensive tactics to attract and retain customers in order to be competitive. And Jay provides plenty of specific ideas regarding how to do that.

GUERRILLA MARKETING'S EARLY DAYS

Since his first *Guerrilla Marketing* manuscript, Levinson has published 11 more guerrilla books, from *Guerrilla Marketing Handbook*, with specific examples of guerrilla marketing tactics, to *Guerrilla Financing*, which applies the down-and-dirty techniques of marketing to raising and using money, to *Way of the Guerrilla*, in which Levinson argues that, to be most successful, entrepreneurs must do a better job of balancing their business and personal lives.

But Levinson's roots are actually in the world of big business. His career started as a secretary at the Leo Burnett Company, Inc., ad agency and led quickly to more senior positions, including copywriter and, later, creative director and vice president. Coming out of the University of Colorado with a BA in psychology, Levinson knew he wanted to write, and advertising seemed to make the most sense as a starting point for his career. After five years at Leo Burnett, he moved to another major agency: J. Walter Thompson USA, Inc., in Chicago. But after three years, in 1971, Levinson realized that he no longer wanted to live in Chicago nor did he want to work for large advertising agencies. So he moved to San Francisco, where he really wanted to be, and started his own consulting business.

Little did he know at the time what a life-changing decision that would be—because, instead of working with larger companies, as he had done at the agencies, Levinson consulted with smaller businesses in need of marketing guidance. But lo and behold, the strategies and techniques he frequently used on behalf of major corporations were simply out of reach of his small-business clients. Virtually everything he had learned didn't work in the small-business environment. So he began devising new strategies that would yield similar, or even better, results for little money—just what his small-business clients were looking for.

While working on building his consulting business, Levinson also taught a class at the University of California at the Berkeley extension program called "Earning a Living without a Job," which would later become the title of his first book. The course was a hit, but students were clamoring for a guide to the marketing strategies he discussed during class. So Levinson pulled together a guide to help them. The title, *Guerrilla Marketing*, seemed perfect to him because it conveyed the message that most small businesses have conventional goals—growth, profitability, and success—but need unconventional methods to achieve them, given that they don't have an unlimited budget.

That one book was so successful that it spawned a whole "Guerrilla Marketing" series consisting of a dozen guerrilla guides, a newsletter, a video, and a Web site. Ironically, the book helped so many small businesses surpass their larger rivals, that some of the nation's leading companies are now using guerrilla tactics. *Fortune* 100 companies like Apple, Microsoft, and GTE have all requested presentations on guerrilla marketing. And more firms will in the future if they want to stay ahead of their nimble, aggressive smaller competitors.

JAY'S MARKETING PRINCIPLES

The guerrilla marketing concept "is that small businesses can compete with the giant corporations by attacking them at their weakest points, just as guerrilla fighters do when they attack regular armies," explains a *Knight-Ridder* reporter. Instead of acting like the well-heeled Fortune 500, guerrillas have higher expectations of their marketing campaigns and use tools and techniques formerly considered too simple for larger companies. The advantage is that guerrilla marketing dollars stretch further, with better results. Consequently, over time, guerrilla campaigns can eat into the sales and profit margins of corporate rivals.

Levinson explains that "Guerrilla tactics do not put textbook tactics to shame. But they do provide you with an alternative to standard, expensive marketing so that you can increase your sales with a minimum of expense and a maximum of smarts. You'll learn how to do what the big spenders do without having to do some extra work. And instead of relying on money power, you can rely on brain power."

Many of the guerrilla weapons recommended by Levinson involve improving tried-and-true marketing methods. Take business cards, for example. Instead of listing only the basics (name, title, address, phone, fax, and email address), Levinson suggests adding a positioning statement so that the recipient understands the benefits of your company's offerings. Other smart additions could include useful information featured on the back of the card—typically wasted space. To promote his book, *The Information Please Business Almanac and Desk Reference*, fellow marketing guru Seth Godin listed the toll-free 800 numbers of dozens of airlines on the back of his business card. He reports, "It cost virtually nothing to add this useful information, and it made the card a valuable asset to anyone who travels."

Other marketing tactics recommended in Levinson's books include standard tools, such as newspaper and magazine advertising, newsletters, direct mail, publicity, telephone selling, and signage. But the trick to turning them into guerrilla tactics is to put a creative spin on them, making them more effective than usual. For instance, advertisers are encouraged to pursue remnant advertising, instead of full-price space. With remnant space, advertisers are limited to purchasing whatever space may be left in a publication or on TV or the radio, but at rock-bottom prices. Because the opportunity to purchase such leftover space occurs only at the last minute, guerrilla marketers alone typically have the flexibility and responsiveness necessary to create an ad to fit the size of the available space.

But Levinson also covers lesser known techniques as well. From frequent-buyer programs to video brochures to affinity marketing and testimonials, guerrilla marketing methods are excellent examples of the advantages a little ingenuity and creativity can have over multimillion dollar marketing budgets. The trick is in pulling them all together into an integrated program, guided by a systematic plan.

PLAN BEFORE YOU ACT

Step one in every successful guerrilla marketing program is the development of a marketing plan, says Levinson. But it doesn't have to be a "Harvard MBA-certified marketing plan. I mean a plan that's back-of-the-napkin simple. Stick to seven sentences." Keeping it simple makes it more likely that your employees, suppliers, investors, board members, and marketing partners will understand the plan and understand their role in making it happen.

The first sentence of your plan should state its purpose, says Levinson. The second should explain the customer benefits you'll focus on. The third should state your target audience, while the fourth should list the marketing techniques (or "weapons," as Levinson calls them) you'll use. The fifth sentence should describe your market niche (the position that's yours in the minds of customers and prospects), and the sixth should explain your company's identity. The seventh and last sentence should state your marketing budget, both in dollars and as a percentage of your gross sales.

After writing your basic marketing plan, you'll want to commit to a schedule to keep activities on track. Levinson recommends creating a 52-week calendar to help you visualize and monitor all of your tactics. Carefully planning week by week what audience you'll be reaching out to, what marketing weapons you'll be using, what your target

results are, and how much you'll be spending helps you see where you're getting the best bang for your buck. It also helps you see where you may be falling short, so that you can take steps to make adjustments. Rating your program on a scale of A to F each week helps you see which weapons are worth repeating and which should be sidelined.

This flexibility to adjust and adapt to changing conditions is one of the hallmarks of a guerrilla marketing program. Because guerrilla marketers can't afford to throw good money after bad, as the saying goes, they devise careful means of closely monitoring every dollar being spent on marketing. And when it appears that an investment is not paying off, the investment is shifted into a new tool that yields better results. Only with a logically conceived marketing plan is such tracking and adjusting possible.

CONSTANT   ADAPTATION

BE CONSISTENT

Just as the key to success in real estate is "location, location, location," the key to success in guerrilla marketing is "consistency, consistency, consistency." That means developing an identity around the image you want to present to prospects and customers and sticking with it. Above all, guerrilla marketers are patient, says Levinson. So they'll invest in creating a look for the long haul.

To be consistent, every tool in use should look and sound like everything else, which means that the layout, font, and colors selected for use on the company letterhead and envelope should appear on the business card, Web site, newsletter, brochure, flyer, Yellow Page ad, direct-mail postcard, and on and on. The idea is to associate your business with a particular look and feel so that every communication which arrives in front of a prospect helps to build a positive impression of the company.

A consistent look also helps to boost familiarity with the company. It is counterproductive to produce printed pieces, for example, that look totally different from one another. When that happens, the opportunity to enhance awareness and familiarity is lost. Or worse, the prospect is confused about what the company is trying to sell or be.

Repeating the same message and using the same look and colors gives your company credibility. It makes the business appear well-established rather than new and flighty. And establishing credibility is one of the first steps to required in developing a relationship with prospects and customers. In the end, consistency can lead to sales.

KEEP IN TOUCH

"While others see their goal in business as increasing sales, guerrillas see theirs as building long-term relationships," asserts Levinson. "Once they have a customer, guerrillas do all they can to nurture the relationship." Interestingly, that doesn't mean treating everyone with the same level of attention or service.

Guerrillas carefully identify their best customers and spend a larger proportion of their marketing dollars trying to do more business with them. That is because it costs much less to do more business with an existing customer than to develop a new relationship—six times less. One of the ways guerrillas strengthen the bond with existing customers is through regular communication.

From follow-up immediately after the sale to a regimented program of contact, guerrillas make sure their customers know how valuable they are. There are many reasons for contacting a customer: to say thank you for a purchase, to alert the customer to an upcoming sale, to announce the availability of a new product or service that may be of interest, to ask for referrals, to ask for feedback through a customer satisfaction survey, to offer a coupon or special discount, or to pass along information that may be of interest among others. Contact on a regular basis helps to keep your business on the customer's mind and conveys how important the customer is to you. Given that most people choose to stop doing business with a company because of apathy, the aforementioned tactics help to eliminate the customer's desire to do business anywhere else. That's the power of repetition in action.

Notes and letters are certainly the most common form of communication, but don't leave out the personal touch of meetings and phone calls. Email messages, audio newsletters, and faxes are other ways to provide information and to stay in touch. Frequent communication also increases the lifetime value of the customer. Guerrillas think in terms of the total amount of business they can do with someone over the course of their lifetime, rather than the total amount of an individual sale, which is how most companies think. When conducting business is viewed from the long-term perspective, losing a single customer can result in lost revenue of tens or hundreds of thousands of dollars. And replacing that customer is extremely expensive.

Communicating with customers without selling them something is another important way to build rapport and establish credibility. A level of trust develops when you prove that you're not just after a quick sale, and that trust can be increased when you offer useful information that benefits only the prospect. Sending articles of potential interest, for example, is a classic way to keep the dialogue going without pushing any kind of sale.

How you make contact, however, is much less important than actually doing it. Taking the time to strengthen your relationship with customers will help to ensure they remain customers for a long time.

USE AN ASSORTMENT OF TOOLS

Instead of putting all your money in one expensive advertising campaign or participating in *the* trade show for your industry, Levinson advises choosing as many marketing methods "as you can do well." This means trying to reach your prospects and customers through a variety of channels, thereby increasing the chance that they'll hear your promotional message, but not so many channels that you stretch your financial or personnel resources too thin.

Levinson reports that his average client uses 43 marketing techniques, but not necessarily all at once. Some programs—or "attacks"—can take as long as 18 months to conduct. The advantage of a range of tools is that your prospects and customers will be surrounded by information about your company. Instead of hearing about your business only through TV ads, for example, they can also be reminded of you through print ads, newsletter ads, Internet ads, direct-mail pieces, special events, billboards, doorhangers, email messages, and fax cover pages, to name just a few. And the greater the variety of sources you use, the more credibility and familiarity you breed. Down the road, those are essential elements in developing a long-term customer relationship.

But promotional methods are only part of the picture. Product packaging, for example, can be a significant competitive advantage if your product can be packaged to take up less space on a retailer's shelf for the same money as competing products. Convenience is another formidable tool, with companies that give customers more time and less hassles being the winners. Anything your business can do to make customers want to do business with you is a potential guerrilla tool.

GRAB ATTENTION WHEREVER POSSIBLE

Guerrilla marketers are experts at drawing attention to their companies, products, and services at little to no cost. One food company, for example, gave away jars of its salsa at a farmer's market, reports *Brandweek*, with the phone numbers of local grocers that carry the salsa displayed on the lid. Not only do such tactics increase familiarity and sales, but they endear retailers, such as the grocers in this example, to the company.

Small-scale sampling programs such as the salsa example are great ways to build a loyal customer base. But sometimes a bigger splash is necessary. Scott Epstein, marketing vice president at Internet search engine Excite, has used several attention-grabbing incidents and tactics to dramatically boost awareness of his engine. A few years ago, Epstein launched a marketing campaign titled "Are You Experienced?" with a limited budget of $7 million. But he used several publicity stunts to keep Excite in the public eye and succeeded in raising awareness by 367percent, while increasing traffic at the site by close to 20 percent.

For starters, Epstein rented a billboard along the freeway near the San Francisco airport for three months, splashing the "Are You Experienced?" question across it. And when, at the conclusion of Excite's term, a rival company rented the same billboard featuring the message "Are You Exhausted?" Excite filed suit against the company for infringement of trademark. This ploy served to keep the name Excite in the business media for weeks.

Another publicity stunt involved a worldwide search for someone named "Dot Com," with a page posted on Excite's Web site asking users for tips on how to find such a person. Epstein reports that the response provided some useful suggestions, but, more importantly, generated enthusiasm among the growing Excite online community. In the end, Excite found Dot Comm, a retired professor, living in Palm Springs, California. So Epstein invited Ms. Comm to Excite's offices and pitched the story to the local and national media, including an attempt to get her on the late-night talk shows.

To some marketers, such tactics are too self-serving. But for many, they are great illustrations of what can be accomplished with a little creativity and chutzpah, rather than big bucks. An article in *Marketing* in 1997 claimed that "Guerrilla marketing means rapid-moving, unexpected and odd." While the article itself was meant to deride the wackiness of some guerrilla tactics, the statement itself is true to Levinson's concept.

Although mainstream *public relations* (PR) agencies have shied away from using guerrilla marketing tactics, falling back on more traditional, staid promotional strategies, their clients are frequently becoming more willing to take chances—Especially when the little guys are winning!

For instance, a recent *New York Times* article reported that Coca-Cola and Nike are using guerrilla tactics that get them closer to their customers. Both have hired marketing firms to employ young people to hand out samples of products and promotional materials to other youths on the street. Apparently, larger companies are learning that such tactics break through the advertising clutter better than conventional marketing tools.

USE MORE OF WHAT WORKS

"The process of guerrilla marketing begins by being aware of all the marketing weapons available, then launching many of them, keeping track of which are failing and which are working wonders, then eliminating those that miss the target and doubling those that hit the bull's-eye." Launching an attack is only the beginning of a guerrilla marketing program. Guerrillas are never content just to initiate a campaign and let it run, as their corporate counterparts do. No, guerrillas want to be sure that their marketing dollars are being well spent, so they incorporate tracking mechanisms to see which methods are yielding the best results, and then they eliminate the worst performing tools in favor of the best.

But this isn't the end; guerrillas are constantly adjusting and improving their programs, aiming for increasingly better results. Whereas corporate marketers might be satisfied with a direct-marketing response rate of 3 percent, above the industry average of 2, guerrillas want to see a 5, 10, or even a 30 percent response. And they'll hone their campaign until they approach their desired target.

PUT TECHNOLOGY TO WORK THROUGHOUT YOUR OPERATION

In the new digital era, customers want, and expect, to be able to do business with you 24 hours a day, 365 days a year. And the only way to make that possible, as a small-business owner, is to rely on technology, says Levinson. He himself has found that technology has freed up a considerable amount of time in his day: He only works three days a week. Although many business owners may not be aiming to cut the amount of time they work (rather, they seek to accomplish *more* in a typical 10-hour day), Levinson suggests that by focusing on "what you want to accomplish first of all, and then think[ing] of the needs of your clients," you can significantly reduce the extra time spent on unproductive activities. Of course, that means cutting out committee meetings and routine memos, too.

Not only does technology make businesses more productive by allowing employees to do more in less time, but it enables companies to be open all the time, ready to take an order. Phone and fax machines make it possible to share information verbally or in printed form, cell phones and pagers provide a means of being in constant contact (which isn't always good, Levinson allows), personal digital assistants organize and archive key appointments and contacts, computers process work and transactions, and the Internet provides a central online meeting place where small businesses can do research, locate suppliers, and market their goods and services to customers and prospective customers.

The Internet must be a key part of any guerrilla marketing campaign these days, reports Levinson, with the savviest businesses aggressively using several online marketing tools. These can range from having a Web site to participating in chat groups, to writing an online column or magazine (also known as an e-zine), placing online classifieds, trading banner ads, hosting an online conference, and using email to stay in touch with customers and prospects.

Some companies believe that merely building a Web site is enough to succeed at Internet marketing. Unfortunately, nothing could be further from the truth. When done well—which means providing useful information, called content, in a pleasing-to-the-eye design—Web sites serve as an online storefront. But you still need to give customers a reason to stop by in the first place. And once they are there, you need to give them reasons to stay, like offering useful tips and articles, and perhaps some fun, too, such as contests or sweepstakes. "Useful information" is the key though, states Levinson. "There's a big difference between information and hype, and your readers know it."

Companies that have seen a dramatic upturn in their business as a result of using a Web site generally do everything they can to drive traffic to the site, such as mentioning the URL in ads, press releases, and newsletters, as well as on business cards, faxes, and promotional items. Those individuals who do visit the site are then encouraged to provide their email addresses so that future contact is possible. Typically, an incentive is needed, such as a free report, newsletter, or contest. And, most importantly, e-commerce activities are built in; that is, visitors can make purchases directly from the site with just one click of the mouse. If the site is set up in such a manner that prospective customers find it difficult to buy from you, then the site won't be profitable.

While Web sites are the best-known online tools, there are many others that can bring your company into contact with customers and prospects. Chat groups, for example, enable marketers to discuss in detail the pros and cons of a product, service, or issue with several other online users. The most productive chats are live discussions of a particular topic related to a company's industry or offerings. In these discussions, company representatives can demonstrate their expertise in a particular area, perhaps interesting other participants in the company's wares. If nothing else, chats are useful for establishing familiarity with an individual or company and can lead to positive word of mouth. Of course, the opposite is also true if business owners aren't careful: "Spamming" other online users with unwanted email will only make the recipients angry.

Email can be a potent guerrilla tool if it is used as a way of keeping in touch with people who have already identified themselves as prospective customers. That is, don't waste your time trying to convert individuals who "might" be interested in your company's offerings; focus only on those whom you have already labeled as potential customers. One thing that guerrilla marketers don't do is waste time and money, because they can't afford to. That's why technology is such an important tool in the small-business marketing arsenal. It allows more contact to be made with people who have expressed some level of interest in your company's products or services.

DON'T TRY TO BE A LONE WOLF

Another benefit of technology is that it allows small businesses and individuals to link with other like-minded firms and people anywhere in the world. These alliances enable a company to serve customers farther away, thus increasing its geographic scope. Never before has it been possible to make contact, and regularly interact with fellow businesses worldwide, so quickly and inexpensively. In the new global economy, small businesses are forging alliances and partnerships with other companies around the world, shoring up their resources and positioning themselves as equal to or better than their larger competitors.

Guerrillas are also better able—or willing—to partner with vendors in ways that their larger competitors cannot. Having the flexibility to adjust payments, means of shipment, or delivery dates can significantly enhance the relationship you enjoy with your suppliers. And over the long term, such a relationship will serve you better than the corporate representative who can only offer a binding, inflexible contract.

There is strength in numbers, and at no time nowhere is that more evident than today. Trying to operate as a sole proprietor, or even a single small business, in the era of partnering just doesn't cut it. Companies that try to strike out on their own, without the backing of suppliers, colleagues, or competitors, risk losing a lot of business. Working in partnership with other firms allows small businesses to stay small if they so choose, but to compete on the level of Fortune 500 companies.

GUERRILLA MARKETING GROWS UP

The success of small businesses at using guerrilla tactics to beat out larger competitors has smart corporations deciding to see what all the fuss is about. Whereas guerrilla marketing was born of a desire to help poorly funded companies be heard through the din of competing marketing messages, increasingly larger, well-funded companies are recognizing that they, too, can apply guerrilla tactics and achieve more for their money. And that's what it's all about: obtaining better results from targeted, well-planned marketing tactics.

To learn more about guerrilla marketing, visit Jay Conrad Levinson's Web site at *www.gmarketing.com*, or call his toll-free number at 800–748–6444.

GUERRILLA MARKETING AT A GLANCE
Plan before you act.
Be consistent.
Keep in touch.
Use an assortment of tools.
Grab attention wherever possible.
Use more of what works.
Put technology to work.
Don't be a lone wolf.

REFERENCES

"Are you ready for naked marketing," by Myra Stark, *Brandweek*, March 9, 1998.

"Author awaits sales results from first interactive book," by Graham Fysh, *Knight-Ridder/Tribune Business News*, November 15, 1997.

"Cataloging for entrepreneurs," by Susan McIntyre, *Direct Marketing*, March 1998.

"E-ticket," by Jay Conrad Levinson, *Entrepreneur*, January 1999.

"Face to face," *Inc.*, August 1999.

"Good ideas," by Jay Conrad Levinson, *Entrepreneur*, March 1997.

"Good timing," by Jay Conrad Levinson, *Entrepreneur*, July 1997.

Guerrilla marketing handbook, Jay Conrad Levinson and Seth Godin, Houghton Mifflin, 1994.

"Guerrilla marketing is going mainstream," by Constance Hays, *The New York Times*, October 7, 1999.

"'Guerrilla marketing' sells a firefly," by Beth Dickey, *Florida Trend*, January 1997.

"Guerrilla marketing tips help arm small firms," by Robert Mendenhall, *Business Marketing*, March 1, 1999.

"Guerrilla onslaught," by Stephanie France, *Marketing*, March 4, 1999.

"Hard to get," by Jay Conrad Levinson, *Entrepreneur*, August 1998.

"Keep in touch," by Jay Conrad Levinson, *Entrepreneur*, January 1997.

"Mastering guerrilla marketing," by Littleton Maxwell, *Library Journal*, December 1999.

"Mind over matter," by Jay Conrad Levinson, *Entrepreneur*, February 1998.

"Need to know?" by Jay Conrad Levinson, *Entrepreneur*, September 1998.

"Plan of attack," by Jay Conrad Levinson, *Inc.*, January 1997.

"Playing favorites," by Jay Conrad Levinson, *Entrepreneur*, July 1998.

"Reality check," by Jay Conrad Levinson, *Entrepreneur*, October 1998.

"Scott Epstein," by Tobi Elkin, *Brandweek*, November 3, 1997.

"Tech advantage," by Jay Conrad Levinson, *Entrepreneur*, April 1998.

"The way of the guerrilla," by Randy Abbott, *Library Journal*, January 1997.

"Why we would do well to ape Mao's guerrilla tactics," by Tom Wells, *Marketing*, April 17, 1997.

CHAPTER NINE

THE NEVER-SATISFIED MARKETING PIONEER

Regis McKenna

The store of the future won't just be a store; these kids will go into a store and want to see and get more—clothing, food, their dry cleaning, herbs....The bar is going to get raised higher and higher; and everything will merge together.

—Peter Levine, principal and executive
creative director, DGA Consulting, in
Footwear News

INTRODUCTION

Is it any wonder that customer complaints are way up at U.S. airlines or at e-commerce sites that don't come through as promised with delivery of the customer's order? It would be no surprise to Regis McKenna, chairman of the McKenna Group of Palo Alto, California, and author of *Real Time: Preparing for the Age of the Never Satisfied Customer*.

According to McKenna, the proliferation of technology is a double-edged sword. Yes, we can be much more productive—get much more done in less time—with the help of technology, but the fact that we *can* do more faster sets up higher and higher expectations on the part of consumers. Customers have come to expect better, faster service and are more vocal about their dissatisfaction.

We've become impatient and demanding. Now, if it takes more than two minutes to get a Web site to load, we'll head to a site that can load faster. Or if we're forced to wait for a telephone call to go through to a catalog order taker—forget it: We'll shop elsewhere. We consumers have a need for speed, and companies that can't keep up will soon be history.

Today, access to information must be instantaneous to satisfy many consumers, because they know that it's possible to get it. According to McKenna, we're in an age of the "twenty-four-hour consumer," who wants to pay bills online at 2:30 A.M., get cash from an ATM around the world at any hour of the day or night, or order a bathing suit for a child at 5:00 A.M. And companies better be ready: Those which aren't set up to provide round-the-clock services will miss the boat, he claims, because this is the wave of the future.

This speed of service has been made possible by the rapid acceptance of personal computers in every aspect of our life. No longer is computer usage limited to businesses and universities: Lower cost personal computers are making it possible for the average consumer to own one or more. Twenty-five years ago there were fewer than 25,000 computers on the planet, says McKenna. And today there are more than 200 million in use. Widespread, rapid acceptance of computers is clear evidence of an information technology revolution that is transforming every aspect of both our business and personal lives.

MCKENNA'S ROOTS

Regis McKenna is perhaps best known for his early work in helping some of the world's major technology companies get their start. He helped launch the first microprocessor at Intel, the first personal computer at Apple, the first recombinant-DNA genetically engineered product at Genentech, Inc., and the first computer retailer, called The Byte Shop. From these impressive feats, McKenna has moved on to become an investor in a number of technological start-ups, including WebLogic, Inc., Graham Technologies, and Real Time Knowledge Systems. And he is a partner in the well-known venture firm Kleiner Perkens, Caulfield & Byers, which has funded many Silicon Valley heavyweights.

McKenna is currently chairman of The McKenna Group, a management and marketing consulting firm based in Palo Alto, California. Although the firm has its roots in marketing and public relations, in the past decade it has shifted its mission to focus more on the development and application of technology. Some of the firm's clients have been America Online, Compaq, Lotus, Microsoft, and 3Com. Many have relied on The McKenna Group for business strategy advice, with great success. According to Michele Lewis of the McKenna group, the firm has more than 80 employees and revenues last year of $30 million. In addition to his consulting work, McKenna lectures worldwide on the topic of technology marketing and competitiveness, and has even found time to write four books: *The Regis Touch*, *Who's Afraid of Big Blue? Relationship Marketing*, and *Real Time*. McKenna is considered one of the foremost technology marketing wizards, perhaps because of his ability to envision future applications of existing technology. By forecasting the implications of new technology, he is able to advise companies on how to take advantage of the coming shifts in consumer purchases and lifestyles. He credits his undergraduate philosophy training at Duquesne University with helping him see the big picture. "McKenna saw the applications, the possibilities, the market; he thinks long, he sees into the future," was the conclusion of a *Forbes* interviewer.

His most recent book, *Real Time: Preparing for the Age of the Never Satisfied Customer*, has won kudos for advising companies as to how they can prepare to deal with the convergence of time and technology. The answer is to focus on building corporate systems that reengineer customer service operations to provide better service by allowing customers to serve themselves.

"REAL TIME" EXPLAINED

McKenna's message is that technology has compressed time by making it possible for us to do more in less. Time seems to have speeded up, because there is much less lag time between events or activities. Processes that used to take weeks or days can now be completed almost instantaneously. For example, instead of having a document take more than a week to arrive at a destination around the world through the traditional postal service, we can transmit the same document via electronic mail and have it arrive in less than a second.

According to McKenna, "Almost all technology today is focused on compressing to zero the amount of time it takes to acquire and use information, to learn, to make decisions, to initiate action, to deploy resources, to innovate. When action and response are simultaneous, we are in real time." But as we've grown accustomed to such speed, our expectations as consumers have been raised, he says—dramatically. Instantaneous results are now the standard by which consumers judge a company. Customers want immediate satisfaction because they recognize that, in many cases, that is a very reasonable request. "Habits, attitudes, opinions, preferences, expectations, demands, perceptions, and needs all adapt unwittingly to an environment in which immediacy rules," says McKenna. Today, watching a soccer match being played live in another part of the world is commonplace, as is immediate approval of a credit card transaction. A real-time experience is one "created from self-service and self-satisfaction by customers. It is instant response."

One problem with doing business in real time, however, is that companies become less and less able to project the future. Instead of being long-term oriented, companies will need to adapt and become short-term oriented. McKenna argues that "American companies are actually evidence that an emphasis on short-term considerations is the best guarantor of long-term strength and competitiveness." As proof, he cites traditional Japanese companies that aim at perfection with each process and product. Consequently, they are not as able to get products developed and onto the market as quickly as U.S. businesses are. Companies operating in real time will quickly leapfrog the competition because of their agility and successful integration of customer wants with product features and benefits. To succeed in operating in real time, companies must implement the following key marketing strategies.

BUILD A CUSTOMER FEEDBACK LOOP

McKenna asserts that the information feedback loop is one of the most powerful real-time concepts companies can implement. Such feedback loops continuously collect customer data, respond to input, and adapt products and services based on the information they receive. Companies that develop real-time information systems will "use information and telecommunications technology to respond to changing circumstances and...customer expectations within the smallest possible lapse of time." In that way, they will earn a significant competitive advantage. So far, most companies have initiated only halfhearted feedback loops.

"The speed and the ubiquity of communication move ideas, services, opinions, and money faster than institutions are capable of responding," he reports. And improved levels of service that customers are coming to expect can occur only through highly responsive information systems.

According to McKenna, "Customers must have easy and quick access to satisfaction, whether they need help with a purchase, a reorder, a check on order status, or catalog information or want to air their frustrations." The best example of such a system is Amazon.com, the leading online bookstore that offers customers access to more than 3 million books. What makes Amazon such a leader is the company's built-in response systems: Customers receive almost instantaneous email confirmations and shipping notifications when an order leaves the warehouse. But just as important, company representatives respond quickly to email inquiries and work to correct any problems immediately. Also, customers can request email alerts when a book by a favorite author or on a particular subject has been released.

Developing a true real-time enterprise will be much like the *total quality management* (TQM) overhauls of the 1980s. Companies that were committed to the principles of TQM, were willing to completely reorganize and reengineer every facet of their business operations in order to improve the quality of the products and services they sold. Furthermore, McKenna states that "Real time management…calls for the intimate and immediate interconnection of marketing, production development, engineering, and manufacturing—in fact, of every sphere of an organization's activity."

CONTINUOUSLY MONITOR CUSTOMER NEEDS AND WANTS

One advantage technology has provided in recent years is the ability to monitor what it is that customers want or need on an ongoing basis. Technology can also help companies determine to what extent customers are satisfied, so that changes and adjustments can be made almost instantaneously.

McKenna challenges organizations to build in a process that "constantly monitors, feeds, queries, verifies, tries, and initiates." In doing this, they will be preparing for survival in the 21st century, when customers will expect companies to be aware of their needs and able to fulfill them completely on demand.

Companies investing in real-time systems that improve customer satisfaction do so, in part, through increased new-product development. As a result of the power of net-worked-computing systems that improve product design, R&D, manufacturing, packaging, scheduling, distribution, and billing, an estimated 50,000 new products are introduced annually in the United States. The benefits of such improved systems trickle down to the retail sector, where companies can restock inventory just in time, phase out slower selling products, and add new products of particular interest to the local community.

Being able to tailor products, services, and promotions to individual wants and needs has endeared time-starved customers to particular businesses. Companies that save consumers time, while still selling the desired goods and services, are thriving. As businesses have adjusted their selections of products and services to meet changing customer needs and wants, they have unwittingly initiated a shift of power—from manufacturer or retailer to consumer. "Choice gives the customer power," explains McKenna. The more companies provide consumers with exactly what they want, the more those companies develop fiercely loyal customers who will come to expect such service on an ongoing basis—from all companies. And they will exert their power by refusing to do business with companies that do not meet their stringent purchase and service criteria.

However, McKenna observes that "customers have gone from being surprised and delighted by marketers' attempts to discover what will most please them to demanding that they do nothing less." Consumers want their needs met "right here, right now, tailored for me," he says.

Instead of having to comply with businesses' limited hours of operation, for example, consumers now have the option of shopping when it is convenient for them, via the

Internet. In response, brick-and-mortar companies are scrambling to match the convenience offered by online suppliers. Likewise, potential car buyers are no longer limited to doing business with the automotive dealer in their geographic area: The Internet dramatically expands the number of car dealers available to supply the exact vehicle of interest. This raises the bar for local dealers trying to remain competitive. Unfortunately, many aren't. And that's true in every industry, not just automobiles.

INCREASE PRODUCT AND SERVICE SELECTION

Retail superstores are springing up everywhere, mainly in response to time-starved consumers' demand for one-stop shopping. Instead of traipsing to several specialty boutiques for needed purchases, consumers are increasingly opting to make one trip and take care of the bulk of their purchases there. Take a look at Wal-Mart or Home Depot as examples of the varied products available under one roof.

Specialty companies can compete by offering timesaving services, however. McKenna gives Pier 1 as an example of a company that is working to reduce the amount of time customers must spend to buy furniture. Pier 1's answer is to offer customers the opportunity to take furniture and home décor items home to try them before buying them. This, coupled with a no-questions-asked return policy, enables customers to do what would virtually be impossible to do in the store: envision what the room will look like with the furniture in place. Consequently, stores like Nordstrom, which is legendary when it comes to customer service, are fighting to remain competitive these days. The service that customers raved about a decade ago has become standard— in fact, expected. Proof of this comes in

the form of a 1995 University of Michigan customer satisfaction survey, which was reported in *Fortune*: On a scale of
0 to 100, Nordstrom "barely broke 80," with the top score of
90 going to Dole Foods.

Consumers want choice in selecting products, as well as
choice in making decisions. Some individuals want to make
choices about some offerings, but not about others. And
some have so little time that they prefer to make virtually
no decisions at all. Some products are being developed to
do just that. A perfect example is a device that can automatically select the cheapest long-distance carrier for each
individual phone call made. As soon as a phone number is
entered into the phone, the device scans all 867 carriers for
the best possible rate and then makes its selection on behalf
of the consumer.

Many consumers prefer making the choice themselves,
however. Fortunately, real-time technology will make an
unprecedented number of options possible, tailored to each
individual's specific needs and wants.

ENABLE CUSTOMERS TO SERVICE THEMSELVES

The only way that companies can provide instantaneous
customer satisfaction is to put the power to accomplish
that in the hands of the customer. And the technology of
today makes that possible. The key to satisfying customers
and strengthening a company's relationship with them is
to build self-satisfaction capabilities into products and services, providing customers with access "anytime, anywhere."

Interactive digital media give consumers the ability to
access information, news, and entertainment from virtually
anywhere in the world, at a moment's notice—and to

respond just as quickly. This interactive element gives consumers much-wanted control over the type and frequency of communication they receive. Deborah Doyle McWhinney of Visa International observes that "the service model consumers want is really choice when they want it, on the terms they want. The idea of self-service, in the early days, had a negative connotation...but now it amounts to service with choice." An example McKenna gives is the process of making a phone call. Years ago, telephone operators were necessary for connecting callers, whereas now customers need only pick up the phone and dial. Although telephone customers must do more for themselves now, few would consider this type of self-service an inconvenience. "Direct access for customers [is] the essence of marketing today," says McKenna.

A more modern example of a self-service system employed at a leading company is FedEx's Power Ship program, which enables customers to track packages shipped via FedEx through a constantly updated online system. FedEx has installed an estimated 100,000 Power Ship PCs at customer sites and has an additional 350,000 PCs in place using the Power Ship software the company provides. The result is a staggering base of customers able to manage their own shipments.

PERSONALIZE PURCHASE OFFERINGS

In addition to enhancing productivity, technology provides flexibility. And flexibility means customization to consumers. In McKenna's language, that's a shift from information broadcast to access. The difference, he says, is that "Broadcast means the dissemination of the same information to everyone in predigested form; access means that consumers choose what information they want, where and when they want it, and in what form.

Companies now must use technology to "narrowcast" their product and service offerings to make them relevant to market segments of one. Although such customization and personalization weren't possible even five years ago, the technology of today has made mass marketing virtually obsolete. Customers now expect—and receive—financial products tailored to their particular income level, credit rating, and location. And they also want promotional offers for products and services they use, not for every product under the sun. Organizations that can provide such tightly segmented personalization will win the hearts, and the business, of consumers who don't have time to seek out the perfect offer. More and more, these consumers expect companies to come to them.

REDUCE RELIANCE ON BRAND IMAGE

One of the casualties of real-time living is the importance of brands. It will go the way of mass marketing, which is quickly being replaced by one-to-one approaches. Consumers want individual dialogue and personalized options, which mass marketing was designed to squelch. For years, mass marketing has been the preferred communications vehicle because of its efficiency and cost-effectiveness; millions of consumers can be reached through one TV or magazine ad or email campaign. But with the capability now of reaching out to individual consumers with product and service offerings customized specifically for them, brands will diminish in importance.

Brand building has been a chief objective of corporate marketers for decades because of the relationship between brand loyalty and lifetime customer value: The more loyal a customer is to a particular brand, the more money that individual will spend on the brand throughout his or her lifetime. Establishing brand relationships has been tantamount for many consumer products companies. And the tactics used to create positive associations in consumers' minds have included aggressive advertising programs, slogans, logos, jingles—anything catchy that would stick in a consumer's mind.

Unfortunately, those tactics will no longer work in real time. The reason is that consumers are getting smarter. They're recognizing that in many cases there is little or no difference between brands. McKenna explains that "Brands had the effect of reducing or eliminating the need to find out about a product before buying it."

However, a new definition of branding is emerging: the brand as an "encapsulation of actual, experienced value." That is, customers develop impressions of a brand based on the company's ability to hear and respond to their individual needs. And interestingly, one of their needs is for fewer brands. Too many brands mean that too many time-consuming choices have to be made.

The key to creating long-lasting customer relationships is to make customers partners in developing and enhancing products and services. By asking for input and feedback, companies can establish an ongoing dialogue that can lead to brand loyalty. As McKenna explains, "Today's enlightened company understands that lasting brand loyalty is won only one way: by dynamically serving customers. Here dynamic means constant interaction and dialogue based on real time information systems. This sort of intimate dialogue between a company and its customers creates a brand loyalty immeasurably deeper than catchy jingles . . . ever could. It creates a quasi-symbiotic tie. The new interactive technologies collapse the space between consumer and producer."

Instead of being a perception developed through static broadcast advertisements, a brand is now the sum of a consumer's experience with a particular product, service, or company, which heightens the importance of highly responsive computer systems capable of interacting with customers in real time.

REAL-TIME MARKETING REQUIREMENTS

To succeed in the twenty-first century, companies must prepare to meet the following three requirements:

- Analyze customer feedback constantly.

- Act on that customer feedback.

- Closely monitor the quality and speed of a company's responsiveness to customer feedback.

Together, these requirements call for a decentralized computing network, rather than a central mainframe that controls the distribution of information to employees. Studies have shown that networked environments encourage communication and collaboration within an organization.

> **REGIS'S RULES**
> Build a customer feedback loop.
> Continuously monitor customer needs and wants.
> Increase product and service selection.
> Enable customers to service themselves.
> Personalize purchase offerings.
> Reduce reliance on brand image.

REFERENCES

Area's biggest PR agency decides it isn't," by David Barry, *Business Journal of San Jose*, February 26, 1990.

"Demographics subject to rules of style..." by Dick Silverman, *Footwear News*, April 5, 1999.

"One connected quartet," by Anthony Brandt, *Forbes ASAP*, February 24, 1997.

"Real Time," by David Rouse, *Booklist*, September 15, 1997.

"Real Time," by Debra Goldman, *ADWEEK*, September 22, 1997.

"Real Time," *Publishers Weekly*, August 25, 1997.

Real Time: Preparing for the Age of the Never Satisfied Customer, by Regis McKenna, Harvard Business School Press, 1997.

CHAPTER TEN

THE PIED PIPER OF HIGH-TECH MARKETING

Geoffrey Moore

The mainstream market moves as a herd....It doesn't just happen gradually. The market waits and waits and then there's a flash flood, a stampede. The company that gets the majority of the customers toward that stampede is the market leader forever. Moreover, its market share will increase over time

—Geoffrey Moore
in *Sales and Marketing Management*

INTRODUCTION

Crossing the Chasm, a marketing book by Geoffrey Moore, has touched a nerve in the technology community. The book has become required reading for employees of many technology companies—almost the New Testament of high-tech marketing—and Moore has become the prophet. The reason? High-tech ventures are finding it increasingly difficult to push new technology-based products from the techno-enthusiasts who are game to try anything into the hands of everyday consumers. Since those everyday consumers account for the majority of the market, gaining their buy-in is tantamount to making serious money.

With new technology products having to fight harder for attention in the marketplace, marketers are attempting to become savvier at getting their products out the door faster in order to grab more market share. And until Moore's "technology adoption life cycle" was introduced, marketers were applying traditional consumer models to explain the acceptance of high-tech innovations. Moore's technology adoption life cycle mirrors the traditional product life cycle model that marketers use to explain the process that new products go through from introduction to discontinuation/death. After penetrating early market segments, technology products have to contend with a lull, which Moore calls the "chasm."

The chasm is a "market development problem that has given untold grief to any number of high-tech enterprises,"

Moore says. "The chasm model represents a pattern in market development that is based on the tendency of pragmatic people to adopt new technology when they see other people like them doing the same." This behavior is appropriately deemed "the chasm effect."

Unless companies recognize that they are in a lull, or that the product acceptance process is not a smooth transition from one market segment to the next, they are headed for failure, says Moore. But armed with this insight, companies can adopt numerous strategies for leapfrogging the chasm and progressing toward the mass market. These strategies are essential for any high-tech company to understand and apply.

GEOFFREY MOORE'S CAREER

Before becoming known for his technology adoption model, Moore was best known as a consultant with Regis McKenna's firm, The McKenna Group. Following the publication of his first groundbreaking book, *Crossing the Chasm*, Moore left and founded his own Palo Alto, California–based firm, The Chasm Group, which provides marketing consulting to high-technology enterprises. Clients have included IBM, Intel, Netscape, and Sun Microsystems.

However, Moore's roots are not entirely in high tech. Before venturing into the realm of technology marketing, Moore was an English professor, which he says trained him well regarding the importance of evidence and documentation. Ironically, he points out, much of his consulting and writing work is based not on university studies or hard-and-fast proof, but on word-of-mouth research and discussions, which is, he argues, the way that the industry works: Fellow techies validate concepts and theories. In addition to consulting, writing, and speaking, Moore is also a venture partner at Mohr Davidow Ventures.

THE CHASM EXPLAINED

Moore developed a life-cycle model specific to high-tech industries that "describes the market penetration of any new technology product in terms of a progression in the types of consumers it attracts throughout its useful life." Five types of consumers—innovators, early adopters, early majority, late majority, and laggards—adopt new technology at varying paces, controlling the degree to which that technology can hope for mass market acceptance. Each group represents a market segment with a distinct psychographic profile; that is, each group responds differently to a discontinuous innovation, a product that "requires us to change our current mode of behavior or to modify other products and services we rely on."

Innovators are intrigued by new technology and are the first to buy a new product in order to explore how it works. "Technology is a central interest in their life," says Moore. And although there are only a few innovators in any market segment, gaining their approval is tantamount to persuading others to purchase it. "Their endorsement ensures the other players in the marketplace that the product does in fact work."

Early adopters also buy into new product concepts early on, but not due to an innate interest in technology. Instead, early adopters can easily envision how a new product's benefits can solve problems for them. And on the basis of the potential for improved functionality—not product reviews or the testimonials of innovators—these consumers are willing to purchase the product. They rely solely on their own vision and understanding of the new product.

The early majority may also be able to envision the potential benefits of a new technology, but they are more concerned about investing in a passing fad. So they wait until the new product receives endorsements from well-established sources and is in use by a solid core of users before they make a purchase. Approximately one-third of consumers fit within this category, making them essential to achieving profitability.

Like the early majority, the late majority is composed of "wait-ers," although these consumers are content to wait even longer than the early majority before buying. Those in the late majority are nervous about their ability to understand and use new technology, so they require reassurance of the availability of technical support and customer service. They also tend to wait until a technology has been accepted as a standard. This group makes up another third of the consumer market.

Laggards are the last to buy into a new technology. In fact, they want nothing to do with technology. If they happen to buy a technology-based product, it would be in spite of the technology. Moore comments that this group is generally considered not worth pursuing.

Although the model itself suggests that the acceptance of a product moves smoothly from one group to the next, in fact, that is not the case, says Moore. There is a major gap—a chasm—between the visionaries and the mainstream consumers that many computer companies never get past. The result is a technology that is embraced by the first two groups, but that never catches on with any of the other consumer segments, leading ultimately to failure. Crossing the chasm between the early market with its visionaries and the mainstream market with its pragmatists, is where high-tech fortunes truly are made or lost, says Moore.

Many companies fail because they simply don't recognize that they have hit a lull; instead, they proceed on the assumption that they have crossed over into mainstream markets and begin investing in penetrating consumer markets more deeply. "The reason the transition can go unnoticed is that with both groups the customer list and the size of the order can look the same." However, the expectations on the part of early adopters versus the early majority—the tip of the mainstream consumer market—are very different and require totally different marketing strategies.

Unfortunately, this miscalculation can cause significant amounts of money to be wasted in pursuing segments that just aren't ready to accept a new product. On the other hand, those businesses that *do* recognize their true position on the technology adoption life cycle have a chance at making the transition from early market to mass market acceptance. But applying some of Moore's know-how is key to making the leap, or crossing the chasm. In this regard, let us examine some of his major strategies.

USE A NICHE STRATEGY

"Cross the chasm by targeting a very specific niche market where you can dominate from the outset, force your competitors out of that market niche, and then use it as a base for broader operations," advises Moore, who makes an analogy between crossing the chasm and the winning D-Day strategy.

"Mainstream markets are penetrated much faster if you have a niche strategy," explains Moore. "Then if you're successful, you can go from a niche to mass market." Trying to own the whole market from the outset is both foolish and impossible, especially with a new technology. But by focusing on one or two market segments, one can win a beachhead—a customer base. Moore states that, in crossing the chasm, "it is critical that you focus exclusively on achieving a dominant position in one or two narrowly bounded market segments," or you risk never being able to reach the mainstream market at all. You'll simply fall into the chasm separating the techies and the mass market.

The key to selecting a niche to target is to identify market segments for which the introduction of your product will generate significant cost savings or will help reengineer a bottleneck. Moore's classic example of how a niche strategy made crossing the chasm possible is Documentum's growth from an $8 million to a $25 million company in just a year.

Documentum's solution was to find a market segment that was experiencing a significant amount of pain, pain that was costing the rival companies in the segment enough money so that Documentum's product would be welcomed and championed by senior management as well as department heads and technical staff. The object of Documentum's search turned out to be the regulatory affairs departments in pharmaceutical companies. Despite the fact that there were only an estimated 40 such departments worldwide, the total loss to companies through the inefficiencies of these departments was hundreds of millions of dollars each year. "When you are picking a chasm-crossing target it is not about the number of people involved, it is about the amount of pain they are causing," explains Moore. The avalanche of paperwork these departments were required to process and file slowed their work to such an extent that the appropriate patent filings weren't sent, costing the company money every day.

Once Documentum proved that it could help these 40 companies solve their problem, 30 of them signed on as clients almost immediately. And with penetration into that segment, Documentum worked to expand the spiral by leveraging its success in one department to pursue positions in others. "Inside the drug companies, Documentum became the standard for all document management tasks, so it spread from the regulatory affairs group to the researchers to the manufacturing floor." Eventually, the company's products leapfrogged into a new industry, starting the process all over again and resulting in $100 million in revenues just three short years later.

Choosing the market segment to target first is a nerve-wracking decision, especially since little information or experience is available to draw on when a new product is introduced into that segment. But Moore offers a "market development strategy checklist" as a means of narrowing the list of potential target markets down to a top choice. He proposes the following list of "chasm-crossing factors" as the most important criteria to be used in evaluating each segment, with the first four items on the list being "show-stoppers"—items on which segments must score highly or be eliminated from contention:

Target customer. Is there a readily identifiable buyer for the product?

Compelling reason to buy. Are the product's benefits sufficient to induce a prospective customer to purchase the product in order to solve a challenging problem?

Whole product. Can the company evolve to a whole-product solution (see next section) with the help of partners within the next 12 months?

Competition. Has the competition already crossed the chasm with a solution of its own?

Partners and allies. Does the company have existing relationships that can contribute quickly to a whole-product solution? (Most don't.)

Distribution. Is there a well-connected sales force or sales consultant in place so that calling on target customers can begin?

Pricing. How does the price of the whole product fit the customer's stated needs and budget? And can all of the partners be compensated adequately based on this pricing structure?

Positioning. Is the company a credible provider (or can it quickly become a credible provider) of a whole product to the target markets?

Next target customer. Once one niche is conquered, will that success facilitate entry into new niches and markets?

Another advantage of segmenting the market, instead of attacking the whole thing all at once, is that you have the potential to "own" a segment. Owning a market segment is desirable because it creates significant barriers to entry for the competition, not to mention making the decision to purchase your product easier for buyers in that segment.

DOMINATE YOUR MARKET WITH WHOLE-PRODUCT PLANNING

"The single most important difference between early markets and mainstream markets is that the former are willing to take responsibility for piecing together the whole product, whereas the latter are not," says Moore. Now, though read literally, the idea may seem paradoxical, *the whole product includes more than just the product itself*—it includes readily available technical support, books, training seminars, temporary workers pretrained in the use of the product, and a fully functional, bug-free product that does what it promises.

Unfortunately, few companies enter a market with a new product that has these elements in place—or have even planned for how to *get* the elements in place. What it requires is the support of third parties that are willing to make an investment in developing ancillary products for a totally new technology. Without customers clamoring for user manuals, for example, a company takes a huge risk in assigning personnel to develop new materials when it would be much less risky to continue preparing manuals for existing software or hardware products. On the other hand, by taking that risk, a publisher can lock up the market and win the loyalty and support of the manufacturer, which can yield big dividends in the long run.

In most cases, to act quickly enough to pull together the necessary components additional resources are advisable. This means forming tactical alliances with suppliers, competitors, or advisors who can assist in shuttling the product to the marketplace. "The basic commitment is to codevelop a whole product and market it jointly," advises Moore. In doing so, the marketer is assured of improved customer satisfaction, and the partner earns expanded distribution into untapped markets.

Without a whole product, a company has no chance of ultimately dominating the market. And without a shot at domination, there is little money to be made. Becoming the market gorilla—the dominant player—is what drives up revenues and sustains profitability beyond the initial blip of mainstream acceptance.

COLLABORATE WITH INNOVATORS

"In business, technology enthusiasts are the gatekeepers for any new technology." These are the men and women who typically work in advanced technology departments—

the group most responsible for staying abreast of coming technologies that their employer may want to adopt. "They are the ones who have the interest to learn about it and the ones everyone else deems competent to do the early evaluation"—which is why working with them early on in the design cycle, through a nondisclosure agreement, can provide useful technical feedback and begin to convert them to staunch advocates for your product.

Because technology enthusiasts cross company and industry boundaries, securing a product champion in one company can lead to strong support from people in other companies, markets, and industries who have contact with the enthusiast on your team. Moore summarizes, "Enthusiasts are like kindling: They help start the fire....The way to cherish them is to let them in on the secret, to let them play with the product and give you the feedback, and wherever appropriate, to implement the improvements they suggest and to let them know that you implemented them." Feeling a part of the product introduction process is rewarding for enthusiasts and can serve to excite the mainstream when the fervor extends beyond this initial group.

Companies need to "seed the technology enthusiast community with early copies of [their] product while at the same time sharing [their] vision with the visionary executives."

RELY ON WORD OF MOUTH TO CROSS OVER

Word-of-mouth testimonials—even just informal discussions—are how high-tech products are sold. "What defines a high-tech market is the tendency of its members to reference each other when making buying decisions—[this] is absolutely key to successful high-tech marketing," claims Moore.

More so than in any other type of market, consumers rely on advice from each other when making a decision to purchase technology; such advice is "the number one source of information buyers reference." However, for word of mouth to develop in any one marketplace, "there must be a critical mass of informed individuals who meet from time to time and, in exchanging views, reinforce the product's or the company's positioning. That's how word of mouth spreads."

And that is where the press comes in. The business press and the vertical, or trade, media are essential partners in sharing information and generating discussions about a product or technology. Moore points out that "the great benefit of the business press as a medium of communication is its high degree of credibility across virtually all business buying situations." Vertical media, while carrying similar clout within a specific market segment only, serve to communicate the value of a particular innovation to that segment, rather than the entire business community at large. Both types of media have their spheres of influence and are critical in establishing a relationship with a target market and setting up barriers to entry for competitors, who will have a difficult time claiming ownership of a market following substantial coverage of your product.

CUT CORNERS ON CUSTOMER SATISFACTION

Although a relatively minor point in his chasm model, the issue of customer service frequently becomes pivotal to many business-to-consumer technology ventures. So when Moore advocates making customer satisfaction a lower priority, it's worth further inspection. He argues, essentially, that you can't be bothered with trying to please everyone when a new product is launched—it's virtually impossible to do, and it can take your focus off the more important task of building a strong customer base.

"The key thing inside the tornado is to get as many new customers as you can; not to create the most satisfied customer base—that comes later," advises Moore. The trick is to qualify and capture customers quickly without alienating the early adopters who get tired of experiencing poor customer service.

Moore uses *America Online* (AOL) as an example of a company that has done a great job of getting customers through the pipeline, but is having difficulty keeping them, due to poor customer service, manifested as busy signals when dialing in. Still, he says that AOL is pursuing the right strategy "as long as [customers] don't become so rebellious that they leave."

Creating a solid base of customers that can be leveraged to obtain even more must be the sole focus of mainstream-driven companies. At this stage of the game, investing resources in attempting to satisfy each market segment only diverts funds and attention from the crux of the challenge: acquiring new customers. Once a company has achieved dominance in a particular market segment, it is in a better position to channel funds toward improving customer service. But unless there is an adequate customer base, there will be no one left to service.

CREATE COMPETITION TO ESTABLISH CREDIBILITY

Believe it or not, in order to sell technological innovations, companies must provide a means for consumers to compare products. "Competition, therefore, becomes a fundamental condition for purchase," and in some situations, you must create it yourself. This doesn't mean actually funding a new enterprise to compete with you, but rather positioning existing companies as a viable alternative. And having done that, you can then explain why your product is far superior. "Your goal is to position your product as the indisputably correct buying choice," says Moore.

There need to be at least two competitors with which you can compare your product. The first is the *market alternative*, or the company your target customers have been buying from for years, and the second is the *product alternative*, or another company that has an innovative entry and is positioning itself as the market leader. The trick is to triangulate those two companies with your own to teach the market where you fit in.

Moore explains, "your market alternative helps people identify your target customer (what you have in common) and your compelling reason to buy (where you differentiate). Similarly, your product alternative helps people appreciate your technology leverage (what you have in common) and your niche commitment (where you differentiate)....You choose your competition to help you define the niche market you will dominate." In the end, you'll be first to cross the chasm and earn the adoration—and pocketbooks—of the mass market.

MOORE'S ENCORE

Following the publication of Moore's groundbreaking work, *Crossing the Chasm*, in 1991, he further developed the concept of a transitional chasm in two more books, *Into the Tornado* and *The Gorilla Game*, which have also earned critical acclaim as worthy high-tech marketing guides. As product innovations continue to alter how we work and live, no doubt Moore will present additional strategies for contending with these challenges.

MOORE MARKETING TIPS

Use a niche strategy.

Dominate your market with whole-product planning.

Collaborate with innovators.

Rely on word of mouth to cross over.

Cut corners on customer satisfaction.

Create competition to establish credibility.

REFERENCES

Crossing the Chasm, by Geoffrey Moore, Harper-Business, 1991.

"Marketing to users instead of to the techies," by Eammon Sullivan, *PC Week*, August 18, 1997.

"Straight talk from a master of techno-speak," by Jeffrey Kutler, *American Banker*, March 24, 1997.

"Surviving the tornado," by Michele Marchetti, *Sales & Marketing Management*, March 1997.

CHAPTER ELEVEN

THE DYNAMIC DUO OF CRM

Don Peppers and Martha Rogers, PhD

The goal is always to understand the customer better, because you have the customer talking to you, because you rewarded them. Now that you know something competitors don't, you can do things they can't.

—Martha Rogers, PhD

INTRODUCTION

The fact that customers prefer to be treated specially, like a good friend rather than just a potential sale, should come as no shock to veteran marketers. Like the gang at the bar "Cheers," "where everybody knows your name," customers long to be part of a community in which they are valued. Yet for years, the concept of mass marketing has ignored this fundamental desire, plodding ahead with marketing tactics that treat customers with the same impersonal message. Granted, some marketers recognized the shifting customer sentiment years ago, but the technology didn't exist then to make personal, one-to-one communication feasible. It might have been possible, but the sky-high cost made it impractical.

When the technology evolved to a point at which one-to-one marketing was possible, Don Peppers and Martha Rogers, PhD, were the two who first recognized the power and possibilities of such an approach. And these pioneers developed a comprehensive program for inviting, collecting, and using information provided by customers to increase the amount of money the customer would spend with a particular company. Consequently, many consider them to be customer relationship management (CRM) pioneers.

The concept of mass marketing has today been superseded by the notion of customizing and personalizing marketing messages and products for each individual, thereby establishing a relationship that is deeper and longer-term than the blanket, impersonal promotional messages of the past. Ultimately, the bond that is established leads to increased sales and profitability, which keep on growing as companies continue to provide personalized service to their customers.

THE PEPPERS AND ROGERS PARTNERSHIP

Don Peppers and Martha Rogers, PhD, first connected professionally back in 1990 at an Advertising Club of Toledo conference at which Peppers, who was then at Lintas: USA in New York, spoke on the topic of "the future of media." Marketing professor Martha Rogers, PhD, was in the audience. Pepper's presentation on how "current developments in communications and information technologies would radically change the relationship between business and consumers" struck a chord with Rogers, who was struggling to teach college students at Bowling Green State University about the principles of mass marketing and advertising. At the time, she was uneasy with teaching students about an approach—mass marketing—that she felt was outdated. And when Peppers presented his vision of the future of personalized marketing, she "recognized a kindred soul." After the luncheon, Rogers approached Peppers and proposed that they collaborate on a book to explore and explain the new rules of marketing. They would spend the next three years researching and validating this concept.

During those years, Peppers continued to speak on the topic and moved up the corporate ladder in the advertising industry. He left Lintas, became worldwide business development director at Chiat/Day, and was then promoted to president and CEO of Chiat/Day's direct response unit, Perkins/Butler. But in late 1991, he left Perkins/Butler to devote himself full time to finishing the book he and Rogers were working on, which was later titled *The One to One Future*. He founded marketing 1:1, inc., a marketing consulting firm, and hired Martha as his first employee.

Since the publication of their first book, Rogers assumed an adjunct professor position at the Fuqua School of Business at Duke University, became codirector of Duke's Laboratory of CRM Research, and, in partnership with the Institute for the Future, was given responsibility for leading a multiyear research project examining the direct-to-consumer channel. Later books from the pair include *Enterprise One to One*, *The One to One Fieldbook*, and *The One to One Manager*, all of which are best-selling international business guides.

Specializing in relationship management and technology, Peppers and Rogers had Ford, MCI, and Harley-Davidson among their first clients. In 1993, Bob Dorf was hired as managing partner of the firm, which moved its headquarters to Stamford, Connecticut. Since 1993, the firm has added several new offices worldwide, including offices in San Mateo and Los Angeles, California; São Paulo; London; Mexico; Australia; and South Africa. This tremendous growth is evidence of the business community's belief in the principles of one-to-one marketing and ongoing efforts to improve organizations' relationship with customers.

CRM 101

Customer relationship management (CRM) is a buzzword that has grown out of the one-to-one marketing phenomenon introduced by Peppers and Rogers in 1993 with the release of their first book, *The One to One Future*. In it, Peppers and Rogers explain why the mass marketing paradigm of the twentieth century has been replaced by the new one-to-one paradigm. "The goal of the one to one marketer is to sell one customer at a time as many products as possible over the lifetime of that customer's patronage," explains Peppers and Rogers.

Instead of communicating the same message to all prospects and customers, the one-to-one marketing concept advocates crafting messages that vary with the individual, based on each one's needs and wants. Then, following individualized marketing programs, one-to-one companies produce and sell products customized to each consumer. Although such intricate personalization was not possible just a few years ago, the development of sophisticated enterprisewide database and communication systems has made it a reality.

Nowadays, customers expect personalized service with tailored product offerings and experiences based on their past purchasing history. And they know that it's possible for companies to provide that service because some already are. Just look at Amazon.com's service that alerts customers when books by a particular author or about a certain subject are released. Or check out eBay.com's personal shopper service, which regularly searches the firm's auctions for specific items of interest and, when they are found, emails a message to the customer regarding the available product and its cost. Both services are examples of customer memory, using messages tailored to a customer's stated interests. Companies acquire customer memory by carefully tracking information provided by customers, as well as recording purchase histories and preferences.

Companies are picking up on their customers' cries for individualized marketing and are investing heavily in CRM as a way to deepen their purchasing relationship with those same customers and make more money. Thus, instead of developing products and looking for customers who might want them, one-to-one *aficionados* are developing customer relationships and then finding appropriate products to sell to those customers.

The capabilities made possible by increasingly powerful computing technology have brought about a discontinuity, say Peppers and Rogers. That discontinuity is a radical change in how business is done, a sea change in how marketing is planned and implemented. Whereas mass marketing has been used for decades as a means of communicating efficiently with large numbers of people at the same time, one-to-one marketing uses efficiencies of technology to communicate with large numbers of people *individually*. One-to-one media are different from mass marketing in three major ways:

- *One-to-one media are individually addressable.* A single message can be sent to an individual or to many individuals, with personalized content.

- *One-to-one media are two-way.* New electronic media enable marketers to send messages to consumers and then accept and encourage responses from the consumers.

- *One-to-one media are inexpensive.* The new electronic media are making individual, personalized marketing messages economical and cost effective even for the smallest enterprise.

Using one-to-one media to inspire each customer to purchase more from your company is the major objective, with the following strategies playing an important role.

SHOOT FOR "SHARE OF CUSTOMER"

To succeed at earning a larger percentage of any one customer's business, you must first know that customer, say Peppers and Rogers. The pair advises, "If you want to focus on share of customer, you have to identify a single customer, address a larger number of this customer's needs, and try to sell this single, solitary individual customer as much product as possible." Of course, the secret is establishing enough of an ongoing relationship so that you can begin to foresee what that customer's future needs will be, in addition to the current ones. And "ongoing" is key.

Whereas mass marketers focus on increasing the number of transactional sales they make to a group of customers, one-to-one marketers understand that no sale is a stand-alone event: Future sales to a customer are conditional on the customer's satisfaction with the current or previous purchase. And by taking the long-term view and considering the total lifetime value of a customer, one-to-one marketers can achieve higher sales than mass marketers.

Obtaining a greater share of a customer's business results in a higher lifetime value of that customer to your company. By thinking of customers in terms of the total amount they will likely spend with you during their lifetime, calculated on the basis of their past purchasing history, you enhance the importance of each individual customer and put it into proper perspective. The average loyal grocery store customer is worth $3800 per year, for example, according to Mark Grainer, chairman of the Technical Assistance Research Programs Institute. And General Motors judges that the total spent by a loyal customer on cars and servicing in a lifetime is in the neighborhood of $400,000.

To estimate the value of each of your customers, you can take two approaches, either separately or in conjunction: (1) Ask the customer about his or her future plans for purchasing from you or (2) use statistical models that take into account past transactions combined with demographic and psychographic information that is likely to affect a person's purchasing behavior. Peppers and Rogers point out, however, that "the most powerful predictor of any single individual's future behavior is that individual's past behavior."

They describe three things you must do to think in terms of share of customer:

1. *Identify your customers.* At a minimum, find out the names and addresses of the people who buy from you.

2. *Link customers' identities and transactions.* Import information collected at the point of purchase into a customer database that enables you to track the purchases and preferences of individual customers. Consider developing a frequent buyer program that permits you to ask for more information from customers, to further develop each customer's profile.

3. *Ask customers about the business they conduct with your competitors.* Not only will this tell you approximately what share of your customers' business you currently have, but it will allow you to identify weaknesses that are standing in the way of your getting all of their business.

Implementing a database that enables you to collect, manage, and reference information regarding each customer will give you the tool you need to increase the amount of business you do with each individual—to increase your share of customer. It also builds in a huge barrier to competition that will be hard, if not impossible, to overcome.

BE A PROBLEM SOLVER FOR YOUR CUSTOMERS

Instead of simply trying to push your products into customers' hands, a more effective strategy today is to learn more about those customers, actual and prospective: What are their challenges, why are they purchasing certain products, and how will they use them? That way, you can assist them in achieving their objectives. Perhaps the competitor's product they are currently buying—and have been for ages—really isn't the best solution for their needs; knowing more about why purchases are being made makes problem solving so much simpler.

This approach is the reverse of mass marketing, which attempts to sell as much of any one product to as many people as possible. In contrast, one-to-one marketing aims to sell as much as possible of many products over time to one customer. To be successful, however, you must entice customers into a collaborative relationship with your business. You must gain their interest, trust, and cooperation—their buy-in—to help you sell them more of what they want. Collaborative marketing employs a problem-solving mentality by involving the customer in actually designing and selling the product. According to Peppers and Rogers, "Collaborative marketing occurs when you listen as the customer speaks, and when you invite a customer to participate in actually making the product, before asking the customer to take it." In the end, you learn how to design and produce a product that has a guaranteed customer base of at least one.

"The only way you can get more business from any single one of your customers is by solving that particular customer's problems and removing the obstacles between the customer and your product or service," say Peppers and Rogers. Learning to solve your customers' problems helps you develop products that better meet their needs, creating long-lasting buying relationships that increase each customer's lifetime value and reduce the chance of that customer defecting to a competitor's product. Why should the customer defect when you've created a product especially to satisfy his or her individual needs?

INFORMATION IS POWER

Businesses of all sizes that can collect, manage, and apply personal information provided by individual customers about themselves have a competitive advantage that can rarely, if ever, be beat, neither by the consumer product conglomerates with mammoth marketing budgets nor by the global megacorporations that are focused on meeting the needs of the masses, *en masse*. Peppers and Rogers point out the important distinction between economies of scale, which larger companies enjoy through the production of large quantities of any one item for many customers, and economies of scope, which involves concentrating sales efforts on selling more to each customer.

Getting to know your individual customers so well that you can develop custom buying opportunities for them may be more expensive than a mass marketing effort, but it also puts you in a position of power versus your competition. "The deeper a relationship you have with any single consumer—the more information about the customer in your possession," advise Peppers and Rogers, "the less likely it is that your competitor will be able to wrestle that particular consumer away from you" (not to mention the fact that you can also use one-to-one marketing to go after *their* customers.)

You can use customer information to pursue a greater share of each customer's business. And each sale you make to an individual customer increases your chances of selling even more: According to Peppers and Rogers's "law of repeat purchases," "The more you sell to any single customer, the easier it is to sell to him again."

The law also applies to communications: The more you establish a dialogue with a customer, the easier it is to continue the conversation and to gather more information. The key is to always be gathering information that can add to your understanding of each customer. Use tools such as surveys and questionnaires, add questions about customer satisfaction and need to each inbound telephone script, put questions about purchases from competitors on business reply cards, and make it easy for consumers to contact the company via an 800 number, Web site, or easy-to-find mailing address.

Take each opportunity for communication with a customer or prospect as an opportunity to gather information, be it feedback regarding a product, a report of poor service, a request for more information, or a question about a product's features. Then record the information and make it a part of that individual customer's record. These details improve the company's customer memory.

As you're collecting information, however, make sure that you are having a true dialogue with the customer and not just a one-way conversation. To qualify as a dialogue, say Peppers and Rogers, an interchange between a company representative and customer must meet the following criteria:

- *Both parties must be able to participate.* That is, both the company and the individual customer must have a means of sharing information; a postcard mailer is not part of a dialogue, because it is simply a one-way communication.

- *Both parties must want to participate.* Either compensate a customer for spending time telling you how to improve your product or service, or wait for an opportunity to be of service when a customer calls in with a question.

- *Either party must be able to control the exchange.* A monologue is controlled by one party, whereas a dialogue involves both parties equally.

- *The dialogue must change* the way you behave toward that individual customer and how he or she behaves toward you. Your company should be willing and able to mass-customize communications, as well as products and services, in order to satisfy a customer with whom you've had a dialogue.

A dialogue can be started with a number of tools, such as voice mail, interactive radio, fax, fax on demand, email, the World Wide Web, and addressable video, to name a few. Using more rather than less will enable you to collect as much information as possible in a manner that is the most convenient to your customer, which increases the likelihood of your developing a true dialogue with that customer over time.

INVOLVE SATISFIED CUSTOMERS

Recruiting your most satisfied customers as advocates and proselytizers is an effective way to demonstrate their importance to your continued success and to encourage prospects to become customers. "Many customers value the word-of-mouth recommendation of a current customer over any other form of information," state Peppers and Rogers. The only prerequisite, say the pair, is that you must first know who your most satisfied customers are—which means that you must have had a customer database that enabled you to record such details.

Once you've received permission from customers to involve them in the selling process, you must find a way to show your appreciation without paying them outright. Payments are a bad idea, for two reasons: They seriously damage the credibility of the customer who is recommending a product to the prospect, and they jeopardize your customer's ability to remain objective. Paying a customer for his or her advocacy compromises your ability to reward the customer for bringing in a certain amount of business: You need to show your appreciation no matter what the outcome, without making the thank-you appear to be a pay-off. To show your appreciation, you can give the customer advocate coupons or discounts, added services at no cost, a free upgrade, or some other low-cost business product or service.

Interestingly, sometimes your best customers arise from poor experiences with your company. How you handle a customer complaint demonstrates to that person exactly how important his or her business is to your company, which can lead to an extremely loyal advocate or, alternatively, to someone who tells at least 11 more people to consider not doing business with you. According to Peppers and Rogers, "Often the customer's loyalty is increased, and his sense of 'ownership' made stronger—simply by knowing that we care enough to follow through [on a complaint]."

To encourage customers to speak up (since we know that 96 percent of unhappy customers never do), consider implementing some of the following tactics:

- Design a customer satisfaction survey that tries to draw complaints out of customers, rather than seeking a pat on the back for a job well done. In other words, push for negative feedback; such feedback is a stepping-stone to a stronger, more positive relationship with a customer, as long as you also ask the customer to identify him- or herself.

- Set up an 800 number to make it easy and free for customers to complain.

- Invite comments and feedback via your Web site or through email.

- Print information about feedback tools prominently on or in packaging.

Promptly and effectively addressing customer dissatisfaction is one way to turn around a potentially lost and damaging relationship into a collaborative one in which the customer works to recruit new customers for you. "The more you can get a customer to communicate to you," say Peppers and Rogers, "the more likely it is that you'll be able to secure a greater share of his business."

MASS CUSTOMIZE PRODUCTS

The flexibility now possible with modern manufacturing processes makes customized products on a large scale a reality. Instead of expecting all customers to order exactly the same product—as Henry Ford did when he sold 6 million Model T cars, all black—production lines can now vary design specifications to create individualized products. From bathing suits you can have sewn to fit your exact body size and shape to Nike sneakers you can have custom fit to your foot, businesses are jumping on the mass-customization bandwagon in order to increase their customer and market share.

"Mass customizing your product or service offering is undoubtedly one of the most effective ways to increase your share of customer," say Peppers and Rogers. And the benefit is that, by designing and producing a product to fit a customer's exact needs, you build in disincentives to switch suppliers. "If it's done right, [mass customization] represents an almost air-tight guarantee of a satisfied, loyal long-term customer," assert Peppers and Rogers. This is in part because of the collaborative relationship that is necessary between customer and supplier in order to deliver a product—a relationship that solidifies with each successful transaction. Indeed, mass customization is "the ultimate form of customer differentiation."

"FIRE" WORTHLESS CUSTOMERS

After hearing so much about the importance of each and every customer, you might think that you must try and satisfy every one of them. But frankly, some customers are simply not worth the effort: Either because they don't buy enough or because they are too demanding, you want to stop doing business with a percentage of your customer base each year.

The Pareto principle states that 80 percent of your business will come from 20 percent of your customers. The reverse story is that 20 percent of your customers will take 80 percent of your time and effort, which means that you need to be darned sure that you're investing your time serving customers that are generating the greatest revenue. The best customers outspend the others by a ratio of 16 to 1 in retailing, 13 to 1 in restaurants, and 12 to 1 in airlines, justifying the amount of time you spend servicing them.

On the other hand, your worst customers, by definition, spend little, expect a lot, and are rarely satisfied enough to bring in other customers through word of mouth. You lose money on them by trying to service them. So it would be smarter not even to try. Peppers and Rogers quote Michael Schrage, a *Los Angeles Times* columnist who asserts that "the ability to identify and 'fire' your worst customers is crucial to providing good customer service." And the reason is that, by eliminating your worst customers, you free up time to spend deepening the scope of your relationship with your best, who are very likely to be willing to increase the amount of their purchases.

THE FUTURE OF ONE TO ONE

The power of technology that has made one-to-one marketing possible is shifting power away from marketers and toward the individual, in every aspect of society, in every country around the world. You can see it in the huge amounts of money being paid to attract and retain professional workers, many of whom have the power to work wherever they please. You can also see it in individuals' ability now to offer to pay less than what airlines, hotels, and even grocery stores have been used to receiving from them, through online bidding companies like Priceline.com. "Everything monolithic is on the endangered species list," say Peppers and Rogers.

Software companies such as Seibel, E. Piphany, and Clarify are making customer-centric relationships possible through the enterprise-wide CRM systems they've developed. The capabilities these software programs offer companies that install them are huge, further distancing CRM devotees from novices.

And in the one-to-one future, "Ideas and information will be the currency. . . . Only innovation and creativity will have lasting value." Companies creative enough to better meet customers' needs will succeed as others drop like flies.

PEPPERS AND ROGERS'S PRINCIPLES

Shoot for share of customer.
Be a problem solver for your customers.
Information is power.
Involve satisfied customers.
Mass customize products.
"Fire" worthless customers.

REFERENCES

"Entire company must apply CRM principles," by Dana Blankenhorn, *Business Marketing*, December 1, 1999.

The One to One Future, Don Peppers and Martha Rogers, Currency Doubleday, 1993

Peppers and Rogers Group Web site, www.1to1.com.

INDEX